A Prophecy of LOVE

GOD'S DESIGN
FOR
LOVING RELATIONSHIPS

Dr. Thomas J. Gaffney

WESTBOW
PRESS
A DIVISION OF THOMAS NELSON

WestBow Press books may be ordered through booksellers or by contacting:

WestBow Press
A Division of Thomas Nelson
1663 Liberty Drive
Bloomington, IN 47403
www.westbowpress.com
1-(866) 928-1240

ISBN: 978-1-4497-5710-6 (sc)
ISBN: 978-1-4497-5711-3 (hc)
ISBN: 978-1-4497-5709-0 (e)

Library of Congress Control Number: 2012911039

Printed in the United States of America

WestBow Press rev. date: 08/27/2012

Contents

Preface

OUR PURPOSE and the meaning of life can only be found by living in a loving way. Love is simple, yet profound. Anyone can do it. Hardly anyone truly dedicates himself to live in a fully loving way. We are all bursting with the need to be loved, yet most of us are clueless about how.

Loving is the substance and heart of forming healthy relationships with others. More importantly, loving is our lifeline to God. To love God, we must first believe in Him, which is a powerful expression of love itself. Believing in God opens our hearts to His amazing love, which is the source of our ability to love Him and others.

God is the Creator or designer of loving. Every human variation is more dangerous than may appear. God is the essence of love. As the Creator of the universe and atoms, time and space, the spiritual realm, and each of us, He would not have forgotten to perfectly design the form of relationships He would have with us and that He would want for us to have with each other and ourselves.

Some might say, "If all of this is so, why has every one of us struggled in the giving and receiving of love?" Humankind's wisdom, as expressed in science, philosophy, art, and theology, falls far short of answering. While the world does not have the answer, the seed of loving was planted in all of us by the One with the answers.

This book is a story about searching and revelation. It is a universal story that binds us together with compassion. It is as if we all have a compass that is orienting us to loving, even while the world and our experience of living constantly mislead us. So many people compromise and settle for just a glimmer of love while looking for solace in desire and the things of this world.

All searches eventually will lead to revelation in this life or the next. If we can be open like children to explore and experiment, while listening to the gentle voice of our spirit, we will learn and come closer to revelation. History, culture, and our own experience reveal our infinite limitations, lifting our hearts spiritually to God.

Of all the world's religions, only one is about God reaching out to us in love, as opposed to our trying to find our way to God. In only one faith does God become one of us for the sake of establishing an unbreakable bond with us and a pathway to eternal love with Him. This singular faith is all about relationship with God and is hardly a religion at all. Some who search may "discover" the form of love He created, treating others the way one would want to be treated. They will notice a peace and measure of joy every time they act in this form, even when people or events around them turn dark. This is a curious invitation to wonder what accounts for this peace. There is only a spiritual answer, a clue offering a glimpse of God.

Often there will be a "house of mirrors" reaction to treating others the way one would like to be treated, leading to endless exchanges of love that creatively flourish and carry people through any and all hardships. In the end, the searcher will realize what is important and what is not—that love is the only act that matters and that it is possible for everything to be done in love, just as Jesus, the Son of God, lived, died, and rose as the Savior of the world.

Many will find these sentiments naïve, preposterous, or unrealistic in modern life. This is understandable precisely because what is happening in the world and in the lives of most people truly is worse than it looks. There is pervasive resignation, cynicism, hopelessness, and an apparent requirement to withdraw and brace ourselves to live in a cold, hurtful, and unjust world. We live this way with an ethic focused on looking after ourselves, which only accelerates our own and the world's decline.

Not to worry. The Word of God has told us all of this would happen. In the Bible are all the wisdom anyone could hope for, the solution to any problem, the perfect guide for humankind and each of our lives. We are told by God to love Him with all our being and others as ourselves. When we do, we become one with God, who then empowers us to shine His light into the darkness.

This book tells the story of someone like you who searched for love and found the revelation of God. Like yours, my story is both unique and unprecedented, as well as essentially the same as everyone else's. I was made for loving, yet I was placed in time, in a family lineage, in a world of lost people, and given a spiritual challenge. My own nature, beliefs, and identity became obstacles to revelation.

My life, like yours, has been a passage to brokenness, to the admission that what I was doing was not working, to the need to do something different. I discovered the need to give up doing things my way, myself. Instead, I decided to find someone far wiser, who knows what works, and then join Him and follow Him.

My own search drew me to become a psychologist wanting to learn how I could live well in the world and help others do the same. The science could only take me so far. Science is operated by people like you and me. It strives to be objective in its search for truth. Alas, people have ambitions, egos, and pride, spawning the corruption of money, power, and politics.

Science pretends the noise and darkness of the world have no effect on its performance, since science makes a rigorous—peer reviewed—effort to obtain reliability and validity. Yet, consider the history of science, and what you see, over and over, are claims of finding truth, later to be revised or abandoned. And where has this gotten us?

We must wonder whether we really have the capacity on our own to find truth. Of course, science has not been wholly a waste. Some truth is affirmed by science, enough to keep us hopeful in science, even if what we end up doing with discovered truth sometimes is hurtful, exploitative, and unloving.

Like most people, I grew up in a family that did not know how to love. My way of learning was quite different from the way my mother and teachers knew how to teach, so from the beginning my destiny was set to learn how to understand and how to love. My life was a preparation for my purpose, unknown to me until Gretchen, my wife of twenty-three years, died in my arms. Then and there we met Jesus. The search was over, and revelation began. My lifelong yearning to understand and love was fulfilled. Jesus had been with me all along, but I did not know He had been there. He had been protecting, guiding, and loving me when I did not know Him. He had been preparing me for His purpose, in spite of my wandering around foolishly in my life and the world.

Jesus has drawn me deeply into His Word, which I had previously dismissed with arrogance. He has asked and challenged me, "Do you want to know how to love? Look here; look in this Book. Look at every single verse where the word love appears, and let's see what you understand."

There were thousands of verses. It took many months of reading and contemplation. I recalled the struggle in my youth to read and understand. I went over and over every word, straining with curiosity. I saw the life I had lived flash through my mind, as if I were about to die. The moments of loving rose up along with the moments of desperation, the moments of love lost.

It was revelation, God's teaching. It was so far beyond what science had given me! The lights of my heart, mind, and soul went on. That was over 14 years ago, and a day does not pass without fresh and deep revelations. I am blessed and compelled to share here these revelations for the glory of Jesus.

You will find four streams in this book that flow together, comprising a prophecy of love. This is a prophecy because it is the will of God for each of us to live with Him and others in a loving way. We can do this now in our own lives, and we can invite others to join us. We will live this way forever with God if we accept the light of the world, Jesus Christ, into our hearts.

This is our common destiny. It is the reason God gave each of us life. It is our choice to follow it or not. God has already made His choice for all His children to be with Him. It is a stark choice, between light and darkness, life and death. So many choose darkness, thinking it is light, only because the dark spiritual forces so efficiently undermine the choices we make about what we will believe, and they confuse the pathway to loving like God. Still, moment by moment, the Spirit of God is giving all of us the way to Him.

One of the streams of love is a metaphor about farming wild Maine blueberries. The essence and form of loving God's way is all around us, available to all. We need only to get out of our own ways, then look and see. Farming can be a sacred and intimate relationship with the land, the flora, fauna, and elements passing through the seasons. The life of the wild blueberry mirrors our own and our relationship with our common maker, the ultimate blueberry grower! This metaphor will encourage you, as is the purpose of prophecy, to see God wherever you are; to treasure the One who gave life to you; and to know no matter how hurt or frightened you may be, He is with you.

If a picture is worth a thousand words, then an experience is worth a thousand pictures. The second stream of love is an allegory about searching and revelation that matches the course of our lives. Every moment we stand at a crossroads. There is no turning back. We have a choice to make about how we live the moment. As we search for happiness, what comes natural to us, and what is commonplace in the world, can draw us ever deeper into darkness. What is actually safe and good for us will seem too scary to risk. It appears we are damned if we do and damned if we don't. What are we to do?

The third stream of love is a personal testimony. Each of our lives is a story about God's love and faithfulness. Each story is more dramatic, moving, and enlightening than the best movie or play. Each is encouraging us to love and believe, even when the ending may be tragic.

The time we have in our lives may be short or long by worldly standards, but against the backdrop of eternity, there really is no significant difference between the shortest and longest life. When we appreciate that all that matters in this life is meeting God, who is seeking us, then we may be grateful for our trials, which bring us closer to Him.

In our own stories we often will find we have common bonds and experiences with others. In fact, there really is nothing new under the sun. We may more easily see ourselves in the stories of others, especially those aspects of ourselves that we don't recognize.

I offer my story with the hope that you will appreciate your own more fully and see how God has loved you and is inviting you to give your love and life to Him. My blessed hope is that your heart will be open with compassion for the stories of others, especially the lost, who invite us to show them the love of God.

The last of the streams of love is an essay on the nature and design of God's love, His will for all of us. What an amazing design it is! Simple yet profound, the form of love designed by God is the same for how He loves us and how He wants us to love Him, others, and ourselves. Love as God designed it defies definition, since that would limit it. We will explore and elaborate infinitely, loving the way God does. We can at any moment, anywhere, with anyone, love His way. It is what ties everything completely together.

This essay conveys the revelations from thousands of Bible verses where God gives us clues for how we can love the way He does and live any moment in our lifetimes by loving Him and others. Just a few of these many verses are scattered through the streams of this book. More eloquently than I, they will speak to your heart and draw you personally into the love of God and a loving way of life.

It is my hope that these four streams of love will flow together with yours and others into a mighty river of praise and love that glorifies our Lord, our Savior, our God, Jesus Christ.

At the end of the book are two appendices. One is a handout I use extensively in my service to others, which describes this form of loving in terms of seven relational skills and attitudes or values of the heart. You may find this helpful for taking stock of what you are doing well and where you may devote yourself in prayer and seek the leading of the Holy Spirit. Keep in mind that these seven skills/values have an application in your relationship with God, in your relationship with yourself (treating yourself the way God does), for treating others the way you want them to treat you, and for asking/guiding others who may not be treating you the way they would like you to treat them.

The second appendix is a handout called "The Heart of Parenting," which I use in my service with families to discuss how we can apply God's form of loving in the parenting of children. This is a map for how to teach children to live in a loving way as you nurture and guide them.

This book is a praise and thanksgiving to God, the Father, Jesus Christ, and the Holy Spirit. I remember well the days of my life when I made God an insignificant shadow. I believed in Him but did not really have a relationship with Him. All the while He was with me, through all the fear and darkness and in those scattered moments when His love broke through the armor I wore for safety, which really was a barrier that kept Him away. He never relented His siege. At the moment I surrendered and was enveloped in His grace, the hurt, fear, and sadness of a lifetime were released in tears of joy that fell into His hands.

In the early years of the church where I worship, we celebrated Christmas with a fellowship dinner and an exchange of simple gifts by way of a "Yankee swap". Everyone took a number out of a hat, then in sequence, could choose from the pile of wrapped gifts. If the gift wasn't appealing, we could exchange our gift for one previously opened. It was great fun. The gift I opened was a Gospel tract of John, in the 1984 edition of the New International Version. It came with an anonymous note of encouragement to receive the gifts of the Spirit contained in this "Gospel of love". It was a gift for living, and for my lifetime that I want to pass on to you. The Gospel of John references in this book are from the NIV84 translation. Other Biblical references in this book will cite the translation source in parentheses. I pray you you will find them just as fruitful.

Writing this book has been a blessing from start to finish. The Holy Spirit guided this entire work. I can only begin to thank God by devoting the life He gave me to Him.

I am deeply thankful for the loving relationships of my life. My parents, Thomas and Rosemary, gave me the best of themselves and all their limitations. I have come to treasure all of it. My brothers and sisters—Terence, Paul, Rosemary, Susan, and Nancy—have undertaken together a great lifelong education in relationships and loving, which continues unfolding. My wife Gretchen, who has known for some time the fullness and perfection of God's love, continues to inspire. My wife Theresa is my beloved, and I am hers. The joy of living and loving with her is beyond what I ever thought was possible. Our children—Tyler, Galen, Christian, Chelsea, and Whitney—stir in us the deepest feelings of love and fear, teaching us more than we teach them about loving on most days. How they make our lives interesting!

Along the way in life I have had so many angels of love who showed up at just the right moment. Neighbors, teachers, and friends offered lifelines and encouragement, often in surprising ways, and gave me hope when I could not find any.

A special thank-you to Nancy Maddocks, who joined me in 1987 as a secretary, became a great friend, and ultimately became a sister in Christ. It's been an incredible ride, Nancy!

In recent years, wonderful men and women of God, brothers and sisters in faith and love, have come alongside me. Grace and peace to Pastor Ken Graves of Calvary Chapel Central Maine, who bashed psychologists when I first met him and said the sinner's prayer with me six months later. He is a lion for the Lord and a gifted teacher of the Word.

I am simply grateful to my pastor and friend, Norman Labonte, of the Safe Harbor Church in Searsport, Maine. He and his beautiful wife Sandi have shown the love of Christ to my family, our church, and me, faithfully and truly.

Although I've never met Pastor Chuck Smith of Calvary Chapel, I am profoundly grateful to him for walking in the Spirit and planting churches that are all about Jesus-worship, the teaching of God's Word, prayer, fellowship, and service for the glory of God. The radio ministry of Calvary Chapel has placed a brilliant lamp at the feet of humankind to guide our steps.

Special thanks to Noelle Carle, my editor, who helped me weed the garden of this work so wonderfully. For Sandy Flewelling, thank you for wrapping this work of love in beauty.

Deep thanks also go to all I have had the high privilege of serving, who have challenged me to love and learn with them.

Thomas J. Gaffney, Psy.D.
Highland
Stockton Springs, Maine

For the glory of God
And
For Rosemary, Gretchen and Theresa
who came back for me.

There is hardly any word which is more ambiguous and confusing than the word "love." It is used to denote almost every feeling short of hate and disgust. It comprises everything from the love for ice cream to the love for a symphony, from mild sympathy to the most intense feeling of closeness. People feel they love if they have "fallen for" somebody. They call their dependence love and their possessiveness too. They believe, in fact, that nothing is easier than to love, that the difficulty lies in finding the right object, and that their failure to find happiness in love is due to their bad luck in not finding the right partner. But contrary to all this confused and wishful thinking, love is a very specific feeling; and while every human being has a capacity for love, its realization is one of the most difficult achievements.

—Erich Fromm, *The Art of Loving*

CHAPTER ONE

The Blessing

Though I speak with the tongues of men and of
angels, but have not love, I have become sounding
brass or a clanging cymbal.

—1 Corinthians 13:1 (NKJV)

THE SUMMER sun is rising over the gently sloping fields of Maine
wild blueberries, glistening in morning dew. There is a symphony
of wind, crickets, bees, and birds that plays with majestic views of
forest, mountains, and sky. The blueberries have lived in the fields
for thousands of years, carpeting the granite ledge in a thickly
matted bed of its ancestors. The animals of the night—deer, moose,
bears, coyotes, raccoons, martins, and mink—have slipped back

into the woods, bellies satisfied with first fruits. Scattered through the field is an array of other plants: goldenrod, St. John's wort, lamb-kill, maple saplings, grasses, black-eyed Susans, wild violets, and baby's breath. Some may see a chaos of weeds competing for moisture, nutrients, and sun. On my knees, sweeping a rake through blueberry vines, I appreciate a divinely loving order. It is harvest time.

These blueberries have been hardy, relentless survivors. Battered by sun and drought in summer and freezing temperatures and bone-chilling wind in winter, they manage to conserve and use creatively what is available to go on living. A traumatic and devastating burn after harvest concentrates their strength in the roots, bringing forth healthier and more abundant fruit after a healing year. Neighboring plants provide respite from the sun, collect rivulets of morning dew to share, and, in the end, pass on decaying organic food for future generations of blueberries. Somehow, everything the blueberries need has been provided. My wife, Theresa, our children, our friends, and I work to undo what men have done before us and trust in a wisdom that is far beyond us. We are rewarded and blessed. Year after year, the blueberries are more plentiful and delicious. More young people join us in a labor of love, bringing the blueberries from the field to the market for the glory of God.

Each of us is like a blueberry vine. Coming to life and growing in the midst of a bed of our ancestors, we have a mission and a purpose. We have a drive to survive, grow strong and vital, bear fruit, and nurture the next generations. We live in the midst of adversity and challenge. Deep in our being, there is a plan that wants to unfold. If we trust and get out of the way, miracles can happen.

> Many are the plans in a man's heart; but it is the Lord's purpose that prevails. Proverbs 19:21(NIV)

2

Living our way seems to be the easy way. We come by it naturally. Actually, it is the hard way compared to living God's way, which seems to be the hard way.

THERE COME moments in everyone's lifetime when we find ourselves at the crossroads of our will. There is a break in the action of our lives, a moment of calm before or after a storm, when we consider our choices and courses of action. Imagine the crossroads as a real place. The sun is shining, there's a comfortable breeze, and you're all alone and surrounded by nature and peace, with two paths before you. There is a sign marking each of the paths. The one on the right says, "Beware! Path of Doom." The sign on the left says, "The Way of Happiness." From the crossroads, looking down each path as far as the eye can see, there is ordinary scenery of a country landscape, nothing distinguishing the two paths from one another. Without giving it much thought, you begin walking down the path of "The Way of Happiness."

Before long, one terrible thing after another happens. A tree limb suddenly falls without warning, knocking you down and injuring your shoulder. You slip, stumble, and fall on a deceptively slippery rock, opening a gash on your forehead. A crazed coyote suddenly appears out of nowhere, confronting you on the path, snarling viciously, stalking with riveted gaze directly at you before turning at the last moment into the woods, where he seems to linger and watch you. With your heart racing, you begin to wonder what went wrong. So far, the path is hardly a way of happiness. You conclude that it must be bad luck and press on, sure that the path will soon reward you. However, your misfortune continues with great foreboding. The sky thickens with ashen gray clouds, the air suddenly cools as bracing gusts of wind blow debris all around, and fearsome lightning begins crashing nearby, blowing trees to bits. You can't find any shelter. Hail and torrential rain pour down on you as you lie with your face in the mud, shivering uncontrollably, huddled beneath the scrub brush by the side of the path. The downpour goes on for hours, and you watch funnel clouds of deadly twisters form and sweep around you. In the midst of incredible fear, you wonder why this is happening to you. After all, the sign said that this was the way of happiness. You begin thinking that this must be your fate. If anyone else were to travel this path, all would be well.

While the terror that you may die at any moment grips your being, you pray with all your might that you will be spared. After what seems like a lifetime, the storm begins to let up. You decide to make your way back to the crossroads as quickly as you can. Because of the storm, you have difficulty finding your way. Everything has changed. The litter from the storm and flash floods wipes out any trace of the path at several points along the way; however, somehow you make it back, collapsing in a heap of fatigue, pain, and confusion that melts into unconsciousness.

You awaken without any idea of how long you have been out. You are unsure of where you are. The sun is shining. Your clothes have been ripped to shreds, and your body feels broken and sore all over. You can't be sure if you have awakened from a nightmare or if your memories of the frightening ordeal are real. Gradually, it comes to you. You're at the crossroads. There are two paths. Each path has a sign. Lifting your head, you read the sign in front of you, which says, "The Way of Happiness." Just looking down this path stirs up a wave of fear. You look the other way and see the sign that says, "Beware! Path of Doom." After what you have been through, you don't need to be cautioned twice, but still, curiosity draws you to look down the path. It looks tranquil and inviting. You think, *How treacherous—a pleasing appearance masking unspeakable horrors.* After your experience on "The Way of Happiness," you are certain this path would be horrendous beyond imagination. Before realizing what you're doing, you take a few steps on the path to get a better look.

As if walking into another world, as far as you can see, there is beauty to behold—lush gardens of flowers and fruits, colorful birds singing, delightfully sweet fragrances filling the air. You find yourself torn. Fear tells you to turn back. Things are not what they seem. At any moment, doom will appear. Yet there is a powerful allure, a glimmer of hope in the heart. Besides, it doesn't look like anything terrible is going to happen. With care and trepidation you go farther. As you pass fertile groves of apple, pear, and cherry trees, hunger rises up within you. Just when you reach for the fruit, you catch yourself, sure in your judgment that the fruit must be poisoned. Quickly, you pull your hand away, momentarily pleased by your good sense. However, fear swiftly returns and grows the farther you go. You are certain that the peace and beauty are seductions, drawing you into a terrifying and deadly trap from which there is no escape. Unable to stand the ominous suspense, you turn and run for your life back to the crossroads. Convinced you made it back none too soon, you rest in a moment of great relief. There you sit, the quandary growing. What are you going to do now? Maybe try the Way of Happiness path again?

If only you knew before coming to the crossroads that someone had switched the signs.

We are born into a battle that has been raging from the beginning of time with adversity and challenge as dramatic and gripping as blueberries or any wild animal face. It is a battle for survival and for our hearts and souls. Love is our only shield and our weapon. The world and our lives confuse and confound us—they switch the signs. What we believe love to be, it is not. What love truly is frightens us away, yet we have a longing for love that cannot die. It is our purpose and our mission.

What is love? Can it be defined? Why is it so important, mysterious, and elusive? What do we mean when we say, "I love you"? How do we love? Is love a feeling, a grand idea, an act of affection, a responsible commitment, tender caring, undying loyalty, romantic passion, kindness, a yearning of the soul?

Love answers the question about the meaning of life. If one were to have more money, fame, or power than she ever dreamed of but did not have love, would that life be worth living? Would not the poor whose lives were bathed in loving be rich?

To the Creator of the universe, it is simple. There is love, and there is noise. There is the meaningful and the meaningless. There is what is important and what is not. There is what is right, good, and true, and there are lies. There is what is peaceful, beautiful, and comforting, and then there is evil, hurt, turmoil, confusion, and ugliness. There is the timeless and the fleeting. There is belonging and loneliness. Love is what God wants from us, and love is what God gives us. Love is God's will for our relationships with everyone. Through the greatest loving force of all-time, Jesus Christ, we have a direct connection with the eternal essence of loving, God. By loving Him with all our heart, strength, mind, and soul, our limitless ability to love others will blossom and mature.

We have an intuitive compass that seeks loving. We are made to love. We are conceived by way of "love making." Mother and infant form bonds of loving attachment. Our maturing conceptual powers make it possible to survive in the world, make our way in society, and find a mate. The loving between spouses forms a foundation and model for children to grow in love. The wisdom of loving erupts in full brilliance near the end of life, as our losses of everything else accumulate.

How is it we are so easily and thoroughly thrown off course? True loving is more often the exception than the rule. Perhaps nothing has been more perverted than love in the history of humankind. Broken marriages, domestic violence, drug and alcohol abuse, sexual promiscuity, teen pregnancy, abortion, and pornography are among the obvious consequences of failed loving; they are the tip of the iceberg. Consider the ravages of ignorance, prejudice, poverty, greed, selfishness, crime, war, and conditionally accepting or rejecting relationships; these all cover a multitude of sins. Stress, conflict, injustice, hurt, anger, and communication difficulties, which are endemic in our personal and occupational relationships, ultimately are the result of a limited ability to love.

Health, emotional, and financial problems are often symptomatic of absent, weak, or perverted loving. Fragmented communities; chaotic families; dysfunctional marriages and parenting; materialism and selfishness; and addictions to food, entertainment, money, power, fame, appearance, sex, comfort, escape, and excitement (to name a few) fill the vacuum of loving.

I MET Gretchen when I was a twenty-five-year-old doctoral student in clinical psychology. She was the nurse for an exceptional children's day care center in a ghetto of North Philadelphia. I was an intern who wanted to learn about children's development and help the families and staff of this center. I had no idea our souls would become bound in a twenty-four-year harrowing yet profound search for the heart of loving. For several months, I watched as Gretchen did her work with passionate care. In the midst of tremendous poverty, trauma, and hopelessness, she was like a fearless warrior fighting for the lives of the children and families she served. Energetic, graciously respectful, bright, and cunning in pursuit of her ideals, she hid her wounds well behind a quirky sense of humor and a generously giving spirit.

I did not understand why I was so drawn to a career as a psychologist. When I was a freshman in high school, the guidance counselor met with each student for a routine "getting to know you" interview. I remember when he asked me what I wanted to do with my future. Without even thinking, or even knowing what it meant, I told him I was going to be a psychologist. It was one of those moments when I completely surrendered to God's will; although, at that moment, I was not aware of God at all. I just felt a powerful, unmistakably clear sense that this was my calling. I was fascinated by people and extremely curious about how we became who we were. I had a deeply personal yearning to learn all about loving and an intuitive drive to heal my own wounds while taking care of others.

Gretchen and I were meant for each other and bound to find each other. She was a beautiful princess, and I, her knight. It wasn't until we married and grew into a routine of living that I realized neither of us had been loved and that both of us were hoping to find love in the other.

OUR LOVING limitations accumulate in our families, communities, and societies, polluting the pool of human culture in which we live, while at the same time shaping the way we live. The drought of loving is so severe that people are considered foolish idealists and naïve to expect fairness, kindness, consideration, trust, honesty, respect, and acceptance from others. It is the norm to distrust people we don't know; to be cautious and suspicious of acquaintances; and to expect, sooner or later, that friends will let us down, try to use us, reject us, or betray us. Finding and maintaining a quality friendship that endures is a rarity.

In the absence of loving, we develop thick skins, put on armor, and build walls. We become prisoners of ourselves, sentenced to life in solitary confinement. There we languish in self-absorption. We elaborate and protect our points of view, opinions, beliefs, and perceptions of the world, others, and ourselves. We give excessive importance to our comfort, feelings, desires, and indeed to ourselves—after all, we are all there is. Others diminish in their importance to us. If they can be useful, we may form momentary alliances. If they are bothersome or competitive, then it is reasonable to coldly use force to get them out of our way. We can tell people, "shut-up," call them names, or ignore them. We can lie, steal, or kill. We can sue people without merit, run companies to maximize profits at the expense of customers and workers, and act like we are the judges of others' worth, capability, and lovability. The importance of our moment-to-moment desires becomes paramount, and increasingly, it does not matter how others are affected by our methods and tactics of getting what we want.

It doesn't help that as individuals, the only experience we know is our own. From the beginning of life, our unique experiences are sorted and placed in memory, to be retrieved automatically in future moments, where they may prove useful in fulfilling desires. The only desires we directly know are our own. They surface spontaneously in conscious and subconscious realms of our bodily and mental experiences wherever we are. Our desires come in layers of innocence and deviousness. For example, the desires to eat, drink water, sleep or rest, regulate body temperature, urinate and have bowel movements, etc., are marvelous demonstrations of the wisdom and teamwork of our bodies and minds to guide us in taking care of basic needs. Desires for safety, comfort, love, fun, and knowledge seem wired into our biology, pointing us in the direction of growth. As we experience the absence of true loving, our desires become increasingly perverse. The desire for safety becomes a need to control. The desire for comfort grows into selfish gratification. Love becomes lust. Fun may become amusement at others' expense. Knowledge becomes a means to exploit others. In the womb of loving, desires develop into noble values that guide an ethical life. In the unloving world, desires are the spark of evil.

Once a desire is formed in our being, instantly the mind is activated to address it. Most of this work goes on below the level of our awareness, drawing heavily upon our past experiences. Our memories are searched for ways similar desires were managed in the past. Ideas and action schemes are brought to consciousness.

In a split second, an organized and orchestrated act begins that involves the senses, concentration, thinking, emotion, motivation and intention, gross and fine movements and habits, speech, and self-direction. The act is modified and fine-tuned as it proceeds, and results are assessed. Choices float over the whole process. At any point, we can do something different, but it must be a deliberate and purposeful interruption of what is unfolding. We can always add to our bank of experience by trying something new to get what we desire. We have the choice to seek out and learn methods from others. Naturally, all of this goes on inside the prison of our own being. Our only escape is to love.

Our bodies orient us toward self-centeredness, as do the social, political, economic, and cultural currents of the world. When we go with this flow, curiously, there is no peace! Not among people, nor within. Common sense tells us that self-centeredness does not work. Yet, we persist. Why? Especially when the only alternative is to love, why wouldn't we all embrace loving with passion and abandon? Certainly a love-deprived world and a self-centered nature are mutually reinforcing. Yet, it would seem the burning desire for loving cannot be extinguished. It is a force that is stronger than it appears. This conundrum defies explanation, unless and until we look into the spiritual realm.

Jesus Christ, the living Son of God, told His apostles and all of humankind at the Last Supper, "...abide in My love."; and "...love one another, as I have loved you..." John 15:9b; 12b(NKJV). The Creator of life gave us the most simple and profound advice; indeed, it is a command for living. It begins with Him. It happens through Him. He is love in both the divine and perfect human form. He is the source, the fountainhead of loving. Like a vine, it flows through Him and into our branches, producing the fruit of our love for Him and others. We can only obtain it by abiding or living in His love. Otherwise, we are alone with another very powerful spiritual force. As it is written in Isaiah, "How you are fallen from heaven, O Lucifer, son of the morning! How you are cut down to the ground, you who weakened the nations! For you said in your heart: I will ascend into heaven, I will exalt my throne above, the stars of God; I will sit on the mount of the congregation on the farthest sides of the North; I will ascend above the heights of the clouds, I will be like the Most High" Isaiah 14:12–14(NKJV).

Lucifer, the most perfect, wise, and beautiful of all of God's creation (Ezekiel 28:12–15), decided to live without God and His love. He turned away and rejected God, embracing a "love" of himself. To elevate himself, Satan would need to undermine the love of God and the nature of loving. He would use his superior cunning to separate people from God and each other by encouraging them to focus on themselves.

Consider his deception of Eve, the first woman, who only knew of loving with God and Adam before this moment: Then the serpent said to the woman, "You will not surely die. For God knows that in the day you eat of it your eyes will be opened, and you will be like God, knowing good and evil." Genesis 3:4–5(NKJV).

Like Lucifer, God gave Eve the choice to abide in His love, or not. God loved Eve when He warned her not to eat the fruit of the Tree of the Knowledge of Good and Evil. He was protecting her. Eve could love God by doing what God told her. It was natural for her to obey God. She loved Him and trusted Him completely and absolutely, because from the beginning of her life she experienced His love.

The serpent contradicted what God told Eve, but he made an appeal to reassure Eve that she was safe. By putting her at ease, the serpent was securing her trust, while fixating Eve's attention on her own curiosity and subtly separating her from both God and Adam. Once the serpent had Eve fixated, alone with her trust, he dazzled, flattered, and appealed for the very first time to Eve's sense of her importance or pride: "your eyes will be opened, and you will be like God."

Such is deception. Someone with self-interest reassures, flatters, seduces trust, and then with stealth manipulates to obtain what is desired at another's expense. How commonplace this form of deception is in all of our lives.

Since the fall, our nature has been reversed from being lovers of God and others to being self-centered and alone. Just as self-centeredness was a deliberate act by Adam and Eve at the fall, when we love it must be a purposefully chosen act.

Infants spontaneously convey their needs and desires without inhibition, completely unaware that others have needs at all. Infants depend upon parents, who manage their own needs sufficiently so they can notice the needs of their sons and daughters and address them. This is one aspect of parental love.

When parents, involved in their own need, overlook their infant's needs (just as Satan tended to his own interest over Adam and Eve's), gradually the infant's connection and emotional investment in the parents is weakened; she will become more detached, without recourse except to look for ways of comforting herself (Edward Z. Tronick, "Emotions and Emotional Communication in Infants" [*American Psychologist*, Vol. 44(2)] 112-119).

At very young ages, children can develop guile. By trial and error, by imitation, and by learning from their parents' response, children can become adept at getting what they want from their parents and others without any awareness of others' needs or of what they are doing themselves. Long before children are capable of moral reasoning, they can develop relating patterns or habits that are self-centered and that conditionally accept and reject others.

One day at the exceptional children's day care center, I was meeting with a rabbi, his wife, and a few of their thirteen children, the youngest of whom was not yet three and was developmentally delayed, unable to speak in a way that could be understood by others. The parents were loving, tender, and concerned. It was my job to identify the child's strengths and limitations, to consider how he was learning and relating with people, and to figure out what could be done to stimulate the child's development. In the course of this task, I put before the child several attractive little toys within his reach. The boy looked at the toys and then looked at me, before erupting into tears and vigorous wailing. I looked at his father, who was holding his son in his lap, and asked him what was happening. He told me his son wanted him to pick up one of the toys and give it to him. I asked how he knew this. He told me this was how his son conveyed what he wanted. Sure enough, the moment the father picked up one of the toys and gave it to his son, the boy's tears and cries stopped. This little child, together with his family, had developed an understanding.

In a way, this child ruled his family. His cries interrupted everyone's activities. His desires were paramount. He had no idea the members of his family were just like him, standing in an ever-flowing river of desires. His family did not know their concern for his comfort was restraining his development. The child and his family were doing the best they could.

The ideal of having Godlike parents who are completely self-sufficient, all-knowing, and unconditionally all-loving is beyond human ability. Our nature pulls us away from God and others, the world dazzles and offers the illusion of comfort, and Satan encourages the pursuit of our solitary desires, using his formidable weapons of conditional acceptance and rejection.

No one can escape this fate by himself. As people pass through the stages of their lives, they accumulate wounds and fears, failing methods of comforting themselves and coping, and growing habits of relating that isolate and perpetuate conflict with others. Truly loving experiences rarely happen, despite our God-given need for loving and our inner compass. Loving becomes, more and more, a foreign experience and ability, to the point where it becomes frightening to risk it. Our signs have been switched. What looks like love becomes hurt. In our effort to protect ourselves from hurt, our hope of loving grows dimmer. Instead of living with absolute confidence in our lovability and boldly treating others as we want to be treated no matter how we are treated, we suffer with insecurities and shallow relationships that grow more troubling and complicated.

In the Bible we learn that God gave His people the law to show them their need for a savior. No one could fulfill the law and truly be sinless, holy, and purely loving. Only by way of a faithful, trusting, loving relationship with His Son, our Savior, Jesus Christ, will we be safe and discover how we can live in His loving way.

CHAPTER TWO

The Blind Leading the Blind

How long will you people refuse to respect me?
You love foolish things, and you run after what
is worthless.

—Psalms 4:2 (CEV)

WOULDN'T IT be nice, before being born, if God would let us survey the earth to find the family we would really want and who would be perfectly happy with us? Of course, such a search could easily take more than nine months! There is no perfect family. Each has something to offer and endless limitations. Thanks to the genius of God's genetics, we begin life with some attractive similarities with our parents and some of their challenges. If only we were all born to parents who had matured into comfortable, confident, loving people; who developed together a strong, caring, and mutually satisfying relationship and who were truly ready and desiring a child to love and guide. What a wonderful start we would have! Imagine two attentive, doting parents, grounded in secure peacefulness, enjoying every moment with you, noting and addressing your needs in a smoothly flowing way, assuring your comfort and contentment. As you matured in developing awareness of them, your surroundings, and yourself, you would feel that all is good and right with the world. As your nervous system matured and your learning capacity developed, you would learn all the elemental skills of loving and how to live well in the relationships of your life. By the time you became an adult, you would be equipped to live a loving life, a leader and role model for others. Curiously, this is the sort of dream no one would seriously entertain. It is so far beyond the realm of possibility.

My earliest memory is of my mother, Rosemary, in a rage, beating me at the dinner table. I was one of those children who were finicky eaters. There were many foods I found distasteful, even nauseating to have in my mouth. My mother was very frustrated. She was afraid I would not be adequately nourished and that she might be accused of neglecting me. My mother was a woman who took her responsibilities extremely seriously. She always had, as she was the eldest of her parents' three children. In fact, as a child, she often found herself in a parenting role, going without the nurturing she needed. Her parents did not know how to be better parents.

Dinner became a time of terror. There were a few meals my mother made that were palatable, or even enjoyable; however, more often than not, she would serve food I had difficulty swallowing. It was the only time of day my family came together. My father sat at the head of the table, eating quietly and preferring his children to do the same. If there was to be conversation, he wanted it to be on his terms. He considered it his wife's job to manage the affairs of the household, including discipline of the children. When food was served that I couldn't eat, the members of my family would finish their meal and leave the table one by one. I would be alone with my mother. At first, she would firmly demand that I eat. If I were too slow for her, her tone would become angry and forceful. Her face would contort in a frightening way. With a tightly clenched fist, she would strike my back, accusing me of disobedience and defiance. The helplessness of those moments was indescribable. Alone, frightened, and at the mercy of my mother—the one person in the world whom I depended upon more than any other to understand me, help me, and love me—I had nowhere to go. I was bad and unlovable. It was the beginning of my search for love in the world.

One summer afternoon, when I was five years old and sitting on the front stoop of my house, I decided I was going to live with another family that lived two doors up the street. With some trepidation I went to my room to pack. My mother found me and asked what I was doing. When I told her my plan, I was surprised how pleasantly she received the news. She was willing to help me pack. I would later learn she was amused and sure that after a day's separation I would return. She never knew how sure I was of this decision. I did not know that she called our neighbor to tell her I was on my way. They agreed to play along and allow me to stay the night. I remember the happiness and peace of that night, thinking that I would finally be with a family that loved me. The next day came with dread, when I learned I would have to go home. It was a sad journey, carrying my suitcase alone back down the street, up the concrete steps, and into my home. At that tender age, I had the realization somehow that I would have to find a way to live without the love of my family. Oh, occasionally my mother or father would tell me they loved me. And by providing for my needs, they showed me as best they could they had love in their hearts for me. But they could not give me what they did not have. They could not comfort the yearning inside me, the powerful drive of my most important need that seemed to have a life of its own. This need plagued me with doubts as time went on, but it also drove me to find a way to satisfy it.

I BELIEVE everyone who ever lived can relate to this story, many with terror far worse than mine and many for whom love's absence was so subtle that it escaped notice. According to the World Health Organization, as many as 40,000 people a day die for the lack of food, clean water, shelter, and medical care in a geo-political vacuum of loving. Many materially blessed Americans live searching for happiness in comfort and enjoyment, while trying to avoid and minimize hurt, problems, and conflict. Yet, each one of them is aware deep down that something important is missing. Since it was not something they once had and then lost, it is difficult to say what is missing.

Just as the womb is the organ where the human body is formed, the family is the womb of the forming person. Our parents pass along to us their genetic endowment, a seamless connection to the first man and woman; their experience of the world and their own lives; and the endless limitations of their ignorance. Through our relationships with parents and siblings, we learn the basics of living: how to manage our needs and get what we want, how to understand and deal with our emotions, how to solve problems and address conflict, and how to communicate and relate with others. Countless moment-to-moment and day-by-day experiences are absorbed and processed by our minds, shaping how we come to perceive ourselves and the world around us—how we think, feel, and act.

Type into an Internet search engine the word "love." The websites most often visited include: Udate.com and Kiss.com, which essentially are dating services; Romance 101 and Loving you.com, which offer advice in sexual seductions; and porn sites. So-called reality TV offers *Survivor, Fear Factor, Big Brother, I Want to Marry a Millionaire, The Bachelor, Cupid, The Jerry Springer Show*, etc.—titillating voyeurism. Popular music, movies, computer and video games, literature, magazines, and advertising are ripe with carnal images disguised as loving or its perverted sibling, violence. Some of America's most popular sitcoms, such as *Seinfeld* and *Everybody Loves Raymond*, portray numerous examples of rejection and shallow relationships, which, curiously, are considered funny! The long-running *America's Funniest Home Videos* gives us one clip after another of people getting hurt. Somehow viewers don't seem to tire of it. On the contrary, our collective appetite for twisted love is insatiable and very profitable.

We are growing in our shallowness and fear. Coldly, people have little true importance to one another, beyond how they can be used for pleasure and comfort. Like a house of mirrors, people reflect the culture, which reflects the people, which reflects the culture. The prisons are filled beyond capacity with the unloved, hurt, selfish, and greedy who have abused others and themselves. Many billions of dollars are spent every year on psychotropic medication and therapies of all sorts to address the trauma, hurt, and loss in relationships. Alcoholism, substance abuse, obesity, gambling, smoking, shopping, sexual addictions, workaholism, codependency, power hunger, obsessions of all sorts, and let's not forget money loving, are just a few of the ways people strive to comfort themselves in the void of loving. Where and when can we learn about real loving?

Going to a dictionary (*Webster's Collegiate*, 10th edition) we find more of an academic description of how the word *love* is used in our culture than a wise source of guidance or insight. Its primary definition, for example, is vague, shallow, or both:

1. a (1) strong affection for another arising out of a kinship or personal ties (2): attraction based on sexual desire (3): affection based on admiration, benevolence, or common interests.

The fourth usage of *love* seems to get closer to the heart of the matter, but it disappoints us in its abstraction:

> unselfish, loyal, and benevolent concern for the good of another; as (1), a fatherly concern of God for humankind (2): brotherly concern for others.

How do we love? How do we actually do it? What are the ingredients? Are there steps and stages? Knowledge and skill? What is the place for emotions? Morality? Our families begin to answer.

GRETCHEN GREW up as a baby boomer in Bethesda, Maryland. Her father was a heroic figure, a lieutenant commander in the Navy who had worked as an intelligence officer during World War II. After the war, he had a career with the Central Intelligence Agency. His work took him away from his family, both geographically and emotionally. He worked hard and provided well for his wife and four daughters. He was unable to find the love he was hoping for in his marriage and gradually developed alcoholism. Gretchen's mother was a romantic. She dreamed of a wonderful life with her naval officer husband, having beautiful children together, and being admired by many important and prestigious friends. Quietly she resented her husband's absence. When he was available, her need for him was more than he could bear; thus began a pattern they created together of pursuit and distancing, where both of their dreams became a nightmare of the mundane.

The second-born child, Gretchen was named after a woman her father had developed a fondness for while stationed in Europe. She was born at a time when the distance between her parents was acutely felt. She grew into daddy's girl as her father increasingly looked to his daughter for comfort and joy, while her mother secretly envied the kind of attention her husband was giving to her daughter. Gretchen was caught in an emotional crossfire at the beginning of her life. Her father came and went, increasingly unhappy in his marriage, and was drawn deeper into isolation and drinking. As time went on, he depended more and more on his favorite daughter to take care of him emotionally. Her mother valiantly carried on with the appearances of her dream, but when the doors of privacy closed, she stewed in a bitterness of empty love and came to see her daughter as her competition. Gretchen grew up without the deep nurturing she needed from her mother and with a confusing affection from her father that was grooming her to be a caretaker. Silently, her parents were stealing her identity before it had a chance to form.

If our parents were unsuccessful in loving, how can we expect them to give us something that was missing in their lives? Instead, they pass along their broken dreams and private turmoil. They go on with living as best they can, slaves of their isolation and the patterns of relating that are seemingly beyond their control. In their souls they ache in the helplessness of wanting to love and be loved, lacking the wherewithal to make it happen. Our extended families, neighborhoods, and communities are poorly configured to supply an infusion of pure loving to those in need. First of all, the demand far exceeds the supply. Too often, those in need pretend out of shame that all is well. They fear the rejection and condemnation that could come if they made their need known. How can you save face and admit you don't know how to love? There is a prevailing assumption that everyone knows how to love. People just choose to give it or withhold it. This assumption would imply that a majority of people actually do not know how to love. How then can you give advice and help if it is not requested? Besides, the wider community tends to respect the privacy of families and operates from the assumption that home is where people learn about loving. When it comes to loving, we should mind our own business.

Growing up without truly healthy loving in our families means growing up with a brainwashing that others will determine our importance and value based on how well we can meet their needs. Our yearning for love becomes a target of exploitation, encouraging a materialistic, self-centered lifestyle, in which we either become victims or perpetrators of the perversions of love. Then we go to school.

On the first day of first grade, I remember sitting at a desk in a row of other desks, each of us with a brand-new notebook and pencil. The teacher drew a large A on the blackboard and told us to copy and practice making this letter in our notebooks. The teacher walked around the room, commenting publicly on each student's work. "Oh, Mary! What beautiful A's you are making! … Richard, good job! … Now Paul, you can do better than that; make sure you keep your A's inside the lines!" And so it went. The teacher was a powerful authority and judge. What I wouldn't do to get her praise, and how painful it was to fall short of her standards. It seemed to me that not only was she judging how I was making A's, but she was also judging me. My goodness and importance ebbed and flowed by my works and her judgments. I was worthwhile if I pleased her and a dunce if I did not. I was learning that other people determine my importance. I came to believe that the way other people talked to me and treated me was the measure of my value. If I made people mad or sad, I was bad. If I pleased people and made them happy, I was good. There were conditions for acceptance and love. My importance was beyond my control. Scary. Looking back at all the years of schooling I had, I cannot count all the instances when my classmates or I faced this judgment. It was endless and unrelenting. It was normal. It was reality. It bred painful insecurity, which I now know was God's way of calling my attention to a lie and the light of truth.

To make matters worse, I could not learn to read the way most children were taught. My mother was the first to notice this difficulty. By the end of first grade, I had fallen behind. During the summer, she was determined to help me catch up. Day after day, we would sit for reading drills. Reading was perhaps my mother's greatest passion. It gave her joy. She understood how important it would be for me to learn to read well. She wanted to give me her passion and joy. She wanted me to be successful. She loved me. She gave it everything she had, but I wasn't getting it. To her, it looked like I wasn't trying and that I was not appreciating how hard she was trying to help me. I may have seemed defiant. She didn't know I was lost and could not find my own way. What she was doing was confusing and frightening me. Often my lessons would climax in a beating. I was getting the message that I was bad and stupid. I was alone. I wanted to get as far away from my mother as I could. I felt terrible about myself. I believed there was something terribly wrong with me, and I would need to hide it from everyone. I had learned how to reject myself. From that point on, I lived a secret life, putting on an act or show to convince others I was good and keeping a safe emotional distance from people, lest they see how bad my heart was. And all the while, I was living without love. Dying inside. School was a great place to learn the act.

Just as drops of rain can accumulate and flow together, children leaving their homes and entering the social world of a school will pool their collective experience about relationships—for better or worse. Looking back, it is striking how great the distance was between the students and staff of the schools I attended and to what degree the relationships between students and staff were adversarial. It was as if the students were living underworld lives with so much secrecy. We banded together to conceal what we were thinking, feeling, and wanting. We learned very well what teachers and staff wanted. With reluctance we provided either the bare minimum, a shallow and superficial appeasement, or an over-the-top "brown nosing" to win trust and influence. At the time, I had no awareness of how living this way was building a believable reality that was based on a calculated distance in our relationships for the sake of maneuvering and manipulating to fulfill our desires. Loving was not a topic that ever was brought up in school.

Lacking the substance of loving at home, it became extremely important to find acceptance from peers. We needed to be liked and were willing to make numerous sacrifices and compromises to obtain approval. When I was in the seventh grade, I remember sneaking off to smoke cigarettes with classmates. Inhaling the smoke into my lungs was both suffocating and nauseating, but hey, it was one of the gang's rites of passage. So was throwing snowballs at cars, shoplifting, and later, drinking and using drugs.

At a boy-girl party in my seventh grade, the host's parents, who, by the way, had twelve children, introduced us to a kissing game. After each of the children was encouraged to innocently kiss a girl or boy, the parents disappeared. There followed a mayhem of kissing, where it seemed the unspoken rule was that everyone should couple up and passionately "make out." At the time, I was a smallish five foot-two, weighing less than eighty pounds. A girl my own age, with the body of a mature woman, much taller and heavier than I, decided I was her beau and passionately kissed my braces-filled mouth for what seemed like an hour. When we were done, the inside of my mouth was shredded and bleeding, but wow, it was exciting! My friends and I spent our youth huddling together, hiding our fears and insecurities. We looked to each other for affirmation, for love, thinking we were getting somewhere, but we actually were sinking in quicksand together.

In the forge of adolescence, identities are formed. Notorious as the time of life when rapid and dramatic change takes place, when turmoil is more often the rule than the exception, a remarkably creative process unfolds. Simultaneously, the body and mind grow into maturity. Sexuality dramatically enters the building. The nervous system becomes capable of adult thinking. There is a powerful need and drive to figure out who we are and how we will live. Confusion and uncertainty abound. It is an unprecedented challenge. Able to reflect, the mind is flooded with exciting possibilities and a daunting specter of the real world. There is the illusion that each one of us must figure it all out alone.

As a young adolescent, I secretly observed my guy friends growing hair on their legs, under their arms, and on their faces. For some reason, the only place I was growing hair was on my head. I felt this was a sure sign that something was wrong with me and that my friends were better than I was. Changing for gym or showering afterward was like running a gauntlet of shame and humiliation. I certainly couldn't talk to anyone about this. Watching the girls around me mature into womanhood just added insult to injury. How could any girl like me when I was so obviously immature compared to my peers? I became obsessed with comparisons between others and myself. I always concluded they were better than me. Everywhere I went I played the role of being just as good as everyone else, if not better, while feeling terrified I would be discovered as a pretender or fake. Even though I faithfully attended church every Sunday and went to Catholic schools and college, it never occurred to me that God had the answers for me. I had no idea that God was trying to speak to me through my anxiety. He was telling me I was lost. He was inviting me to join Him. He loved me and wanted me to love Him.

SCHOOLING CERTAINLY leaves us with the impression that our worth and value are determined by our achievements. Implicit judgments are made about people in terms of how far they went in their education, how well they did, and how difficult or challenging their course of study was. Doctors and lawyers are considered better than mere college graduates, who are better than people with a high school education, and so on. It stands to reason that the doctors and lawyers deserve greater reward for their accomplishments. Professional athletes, movie stars, popular musicians, artists, cultural icons, the captains of big business, and political and church leaders enjoy an exalted status, with power and freedoms that proclaim they are better than "the little people." It is curious that when Jesus walked the earth, he turned away from "the better people" and embraced the ordinary and rejected.

The world and our local communities seamlessly pick up where our educational communities leave off, only with greater detachment and violence. By the time we step into our adult lives and "the real world," social forces acquire critical mass. As individuals, each of us is for the most part alone, concerned with survival and our own lives. There are powerful incentives to join the club or status quo, to conform or pay dearly. The pronouns *I* and *me* far outnumber *we*. When *we* appears on the radar screen, quite often it serves the agenda of an individual or group of individuals, each seeking achievements or status. This culture brainwashes our day-to-day lives, valuing, or shall we say worshiping, materialism, comfort, pleasure, power, status, fame, "success," and self. The carnage of cruelty, selfishness, and greed proliferates. Our media hold the mirror of this "reality," further shaping what we believe and how we treat each other. With appalling rarity of kindness, friendship, and love, our civilization is racing for the cliff like lemmings.

With the backdrop of a competitive and uncaring world, an inner life of uncertainty and loneliness, and a powerful natural drive for loving, is it any wonder that early and often we go looking for a mate? In the animal kingdom, the usual course of life is to grow into maturity, obtain experience and strength, and then look for a mate. Human beings, with their big brains and sophistication, may be the only species that goes looking for mates before reaching maturity, unprepared for the potential responsibility of conception. We look for mates in desperate hope of finding someone who can complete us, who can heal us, who can love us. If we don't feel important, we must find someone who will prove we are. If we are afraid and insecure, we will look for someone we can depend upon to protect us, who will never leave. If we are lonely, the urge to merge may overtake us and eventually drive away anyone who enters our intimate orbit. If we feel fulfilled giving to another in hopes that we will be desired, we will likely be running on empty before the other runs out of desires. There seems to be an unlimited number of ways that love can go awry. It is a common story, beginning in adolescence, that people ride an emotional roller coaster of romantic highs and painful losses as they search for a love that can endure and satisfy. It seems like it is a matter of finding the right person. We are not accustomed to looking deeper. Who would think there might be something critical missing?

Usually after a series of disappointing relationships, after waiting longer than we can stand, we are ready to fool ourselves into believing the next one is the one! We will idealize or idolize this unsuspecting person who may also be doing the same thing to us. It seems so perfect, so right, so fulfilling of all we ever dreamed loving would be. Naturally, we must say "I do" and begin living happily ever after, only to find out a short time later that there was much more to the person we loved than we ever imagined. How could we have missed it? Answer: we were too busy creating a fantasy and seducing to notice. Our perfect love was of our own making. As the truth comes into focus, distance begins growing, and the relationship increasingly becomes work. Of course, our relatives and friends warned us about this. Some soldier on, some begin leaving, and some decide to have children.

Having children may be the ultimate romance: our own little creature, cute, cuddly, totally in awe and in love with us. With our children, we finally get a chance to do it right. Starting with a blank slate, we will protect them, take care of them, nurture and love them, and teach them everything they need to know. We will dress them in darling clothes, show off their beautiful curls, shower them with hugs, kisses, and attention, bounce them on our knees, teach them delightful songs, and laugh at their silly antics. Come to think of it, we can treat them the way we always wanted to be treated! They shall be princes and princesses. They will reward us with great pleasure and gratitude.

One problem. As time goes on, children have a habit of becoming their own unique people. They can't help it. It is, in fact, impossible for them to become who we would like them to be. Like us, they will need to find their own way, make their own choices. It is only a matter of time before conflict between what we want and what they want lets the air out of the romantic balloon. Then comes a darker cynicism as we approach the resignation that our hopes for loving will not be fulfilled. At home, our children are introduced to the darkness of the world. And so it goes. The blind leading the blind.

> Whoever would love life and see good days must keep his tongue from evil and his lips from deceitful speech. He must turn from evil and do good; he must seek peace and pursue it. 1 Peter 3:10, 11(NIV)

CHAPTER THREE

The Heart of Darkness

A man who isolates himself seeks his own desire;
he rages against all wise judgment.

—Proverbs 18:1 (NKJV)

IN MAINE, between the liberating warmth of summer and the
dark, hard cold of winter, is the short, brilliantly colorful season
of fall. This is a time to say goodbye to summer and begin bracing
for winter. The light of fall has a unique beauty. At sunrise, the
sky is brushed and glowing with soft rose colors, muted blue, and
mauve, with etchings of bright yellow light finding its way through
soft, puffy clouds. The light of the morning seems clean, pure, and
fresh. The afternoons are radiant in sepia, stirring up memories
of freshly baked bread, stacking firewood with the children, and

walking hand in hand with my love through autumn woods. At the close of the day, scarlet, pastel orange, and blue swirl around the setting sun. Standing still in quiet awe, peacefulness sweeps away the day's debris. Then darkness comes.

In the blueberry fields, fall is a time for cleaning up after the harvest and preparing for spring. The string laid out in the field to guide the rakers is gathered up, along with forgotten water bottles and clothing left in the burning sun, testaments of wandering minds in labor. In bracing winds, I walk the fields, cutting the stalks of maple, poplar, birch, and ash that sprout up relentlessly from sturdy roots. Somewhere else, these trees would grow, exchanging oxygen for carbon dioxide, offering shelter and shade to creatures of all sorts, rising up to contribute their colors in the fall, or perhaps being sacrificed to warm the homes of families in winter. Here their power would overwhelm the blueberries, consuming precious sun, water, and nutrients. The process of weeding separates what is important and what is not. The work sets me weeding my own mind and life.

Between the nor'easters of November, on a calm steely day, the tractors come pulling their monstrous burners to scorch the vines and blacken the fields. A lush carpet of scarlet beauty becomes a haunting landscape of hell. Just below the surface, the roots of the blueberry vines recoil in shock, seal in their energy, and preserve their lives and plans for resurrection in the spring to grow stronger and, a year later, bear more fruit. Blankets of snow soon cover the burn. Bitter cold and biting winds freeze the ground four feet down. Days with sixteen hours of darkness descend over all, scattering hope.

AT THE crossroads, discouragement prevails. The Way of Happiness and the Path of Doom are equally ominous. There is no turning back, a yearning to move on, and a foreboding that no matter what the choice, suffering is coming. You recall the words of an old friend: "In life we choose the way we suffer." The helplessness of standing at the crossroads moves you to try again. You have to do something. With great trepidation, you set off down the Way of Happiness. A profound cold and dark envelops you, alone with pure fear.

AS JESUS approached the city of Jerusalem on the back of a colt, amid His jubilant welcome as the Messiah, He said, "If you had known, even you, especially in this your day, the things that make for your peace! But now they are hidden from your eyes. For days will come upon you when your enemies will build an embankment around you, surround you and close you in on every side, and level you, and your children within you, to the ground; and they will not leave in you one stone upon another, because you did not know the time of your visitation." Luke 19:42–44(NKJV)

He knew what was coming. The rejection of humankind, past, present, and future, was concentrating and intensifying. In just five days, Jesus would step alone into a great fury of hatred and evil. His enemy was anticipating a crushing victory. There was no escape. God was contained in the flesh and blood of a man. Death was approaching with horrendous cruelty. The friends of Jesus would abandon Him in fear; for the only time in eternity He would be alone and separate from His Father. Moved by love for His Father and us, He entered the heart of darkness.

Gretchen's mother and father believed she would be a wonderful nurse. She was bright, sensitive, caring, and energetic. As loving parents, they were prepared to encourage her to go to college and to make sacrifices for her higher education. They did not know how each of them was grooming Gretchen to become their caretaker.

Mother needed Gretchen to prove what a remarkable mother she was. A deep fear of rejection and loneliness prompted Mother to accept Gretchen on the condition that she would please her. This required Gretchen to be attentive to her mother's wishes and dislikes, while increasingly distrusting her own preferences. Mother was teaching Gretchen that her value and worth depended upon her works and her ability to please others. Self-sacrifice was reverenced very highly by Mother, but it was rarely modeled in action.

Father was looking to Gretchen for what he could not find in his marriage. He was a playful fellow who found intimacy in secrets, mischief, and shared pleasures. The demands on his time, the responsibilities of career and family, and his unfulfilling marriage drew him to find comfort in alcohol, and his daughter. For Gretchen, his attention was as confusing as it was intermittent. At times she was a princess lavished with favors. At other times she was coldly pressured for favors. What was clear was that if she pleased him, he would love her. The price she paid for his love was the betrayal of herself.

Dutifully, Gretchen pleased her parents and became the person they wanted her to be: a nurse with a college degree and an officer's commission in the Navy. She had thought this would secure their love. Actually, it was the beginning of a nightmare that eventually would take her life.

Two years after I married Gretchen, I was sitting alone in the office of a psychologist who had completed an evaluation of my wife, who had begun sinking into depression and alcoholism. She was on the verge of being fired from her job as a public health nurse. The doctor told me there was not much hope. He could not say how, but my wife had been severely hurt. He did not think she could recover. His words stunned me. I could not absorb what this meant. I left his office with Gretchen, dazed. I had to keep what he said to myself. I put my arm around her as we walked to the car in silence, wishing somehow my love could heal her. My shock was like a fog that lifted as I meditated on one of my marriage vows to love her forever. I was determined to find a way to save her life.

We decided together to leave Philadelphia and move to a small community where we could simplify our lives and give Gretchen a chance to find herself. I took a job as a psychologist in the St. John Valley of northern Maine. Gretchen would no longer need to work as a nurse and could return to college and obtain a degree in one of her passions, environmental science. Along the way she would also discover several of her brilliant talents, including art, writing, and photography. Getting from our complicated and stress-filled urban life to a rural Acadian community proved to be traumatic, as would be every significant change in our lives.

I went ahead and started my job in November, leaving Gretchen behind in Philadelphia to complete the sale of our home. I looked for a place we could rent, so we could take our time to decide where we would like to settle. Alone, Gretchen had a harrowing time dealing with the fellow who eventually bought our home. He would drop in unannounced with a video camera and friends, wanting to go through the home. He insisted on having dinner with Gretchen to discuss endless details of the purchase. The deal was on and off, based on his whims. She was helplessly riding an emotional roller coaster, while I was seven hundred miles away. For her sake, I insisted she join me before the deal was complete. She arrived in a strange new world that was forty degrees below zero, with three feet of snow on the ground. With all our worldly belongings in a moving van driven by a sleazy character, who insisted on staying the night with us before unloading the truck, Gretchen was teetering on the edge of sanity. Her moods shifted wildly; one moment she was tearfully happy and overjoyed to be with me again; then she was cynical, restless, and hostile the next. In the first few weeks, she was withdrawn, distant, and brooding, spending most of her time alone, struggling to make the house we were renting her home. Occasionally, she would dress eccentrically, with clashing layers of clothing and leggings that went up to her crotch, and she would make up her face cartoonishly with bright rouge, deep red lipstick, and thick mascara. Then she would walk about the town. She was frightened, confused, and in turmoil. Nothing I did seemed to help. We soon learned that our empty home in Philadelphia was burglarized and vandalized. With all of this as a backdrop, Gretchen drove to town on an errand, leaving her beloved West Highland terrier, Britt, outside untethered.

Before we were married, Gretchen had told me that when she was a little girl she had always dreamed someday of having her own West Highland terrier. I did not know then how she had fantasized that this cute, spirited dog would be an object of love and comfort that would be with her through her emotional ordeals and how she had so personally identified with it. I only knew it would mean a great deal to her if I could fulfill this dream. I gave her Britt as my wedding present. She became a delightful and endearing joy in our lives. For Gretchen, Britt was her child. Britt was Gretchen.

In the early afternoon while I was in a counseling session, my secretary interrupted the meeting, telling me my mother-in-law was on the phone in an emotionally hysterical state. I excused myself, and took the call. Lucy was wailing with emotional urgency and barely understandable. Something was desperately wrong with Gretchen and it had something to do with Britt. It never occurred to me to call for help. Single-mindedly I went to her as fast as I could. When I walked through the door, I found her broken, sobbing uncontrollably on the floor. I lay down with her, put my arm around her, and she told me through her agony, Britt was dead. Time stopped. We lay on the floor holding each other, our tears flowing together until we couldn't cry anymore. Britt had run after Gretchen as she drove away and was struck by a following car that continued on after killing her. Gretchen saw it all through the rearview mirror. Beside herself with trauma, she left her car, carried Britt's lifeless body back to the house, called her mother, and collapsed in grief. Two weeks later, Gretchen was hospitalized. All she wanted to do was die.

In different ways, Gretchen and I were being consumed in a fire of darkness and helplessness. She was in a pain I could not imagine. I was powerless to comfort her. She could see no end to her misery. No hope. So far, my attempts to save her were disastrous. But, this was only the beginning. The climax was seventeen years away.

WITH HIS desire for loving, God created the angels and humankind with free will. After all, wouldn't love be shallow without it? What satisfaction could there be in loving that is totally controlled? It would be nothing more than a phony love of self. Can you imagine God using his infinite power to direct all His creation to worship Him on cue? It is absurd.

Before the universe was created, the eternal God gave immortal life to the angels for a loving relationship with Him. The moment of their creation must have been extraordinary beyond our understanding. As humans we grow into consciousness over a period of years, gradually understanding more and more about ourselves, the people around us, and the world. We do not know if God created the angels in a moment, as He created Adam, or if His creation was like a conception, followed by a gradual course of growth—something like our own lives. Between the two possibilities, it seems more likely God would have created the angels as He created Adam: one moment, nothing; the next, a complete living being. It was not until after the fall that humankind would come to life through the ordeal of childbirth.

Anyone who has children will likely never forget the first moment she looked upon her newborn child and held him in her arms. It is a moment of awe, joy, incredible love, and a fierce desire to protect. How God must also have treasured the moment He first beheld His loving creation! He must have especially treasured it if His angels could appreciate the significance of the moment as they looked into the eyes of their Almighty Father God, who made them to receive His love and love Him in return. The process of a developing human attachment between mother and infant perhaps gives us a clue about the glorious ecstasy of that moment.

The afterglow of coming into existence at the hands of God could have been no less remarkable. For a moment, pretend you were one of these angels. As the light of living goes on, your being is filled with perfect peace and love. You know with absolute clarity your purpose for being is to be loved by the Creator of the universe and to love Him without end. The joy would be indescribable. Thankfulness would be delirious, yet humbling. The heartfelt yearning to praise, worship, and serve Him would be all-consuming. To witness His delight in your love of Him would be intensely affirming and almost unbearably sweet. As He loved you, inspiration and motivation for loving Him would grow by leaps and bounds. It would probably be eons before it would occur to you that there was any other way to be.

But surely that moment would also come. In the glory of God's love the angels would come to share a great love for one another. The common ground of being loved by God and loving Him would naturally orient them to love each other. As time passed, the angels would come to know each other, and in the reflection of their relationships with God and each other, they would also come to know themselves. They would notice each other's uniqueness, which in the context of their loving, would be a cause for celebrating the glory of God. Inevitably, one angel would discover the other choice in the midst of these comparisons.

We are told in the Bible, Lucifer was the most awesome and magnificent creature God ever created (Ezekiel 28:12–15). He enjoyed an elite status with God, endowed with brilliance and power beyond the other angels; he was given a special blessing from God, and a special challenge, as surely he was among the first of God's creatures to discover free will.

As Lucifer noticed the differences between himself and God, and himself and the other angels, his attention increasingly drifted away from God, and to himself. Fully aware of what he was doing, he deliberately turned away from God's love and, for the first time, completely perverted loving by becoming his own object of worship, his own god. He assumed powers that belonged only to God. He considered himself the ultimate judge, accepting only angels who would follow him, while rejecting with determination to destroy any who would oppose him. We are told that in his revolt, one third of the angels were cast down from heaven to the earth with Satan, where they have continued the battle to pervert and destroy the love of God and love itself. In the spiritual realm, our lives are the battlefield.

Moment by moment, day by day, we pursue our desires surrounded by others pursuing their desires. We can ignore what others want and single-mindedly try to fulfill our desires, or we may sacrifice what we want, allowing others to have their way in an attempt to keep the peace. On the face of it, there appears to be only two choices to fulfill desires. I can become a taker, who by virtue of past conflicts comes to believe that people are basically self-interested and cannot be trusted to care about me. Therefore, realizing this harsh reality, the only way of living in relationships that makes any sense is to take care of myself. I become more important than other people. How I choose to fulfill my desires is justifiable, regardless of the consequences to others, because they are not as important as I am. My satisfaction and comfort justifies the means I use to obtain it. Anyone else who lives differently is a fool and an inviting target for abuse and use. If I am a taker, relationships will be stable as long as other people help me have what I want. People are loving if they provide what I want. People who don't are bad and mean. They deserve to be treated punitively. Everything would be wonderful if only other people were nice to me and gave me what I want.

Givers hope to obtain what they want by way of pleasing others or, in other words, going out of their way to notice what others want and providing it, no matter what the cost. Givers do not want to hurt others or be hurt by others, so enormous importance is given to reducing conflict and keeping the peace. Givers learn that as long as others are happy and getting what they want, peace can be maintained. It is worth sacrificing their own desires for the sake of peace. In fact, it is good and they are good if they deny themselves for the sake of others. Givers look at the world much like takers in one respect; they both expect that people are more likely to hurt than care. They have completely opposite ways of protecting themselves; the taker only gives importance to herself, and the giver only gives importance to others.

While it is true that there are people who are sometimes takers and sometimes givers, for the most part each of us develops a primary relating style. There are, of course, degrees of giving and taking. Some takers may resort to innocent manipulation for the sake of comfort, while others can resort to murder. The sacrifices of some givers may be so modest as to be inconsequential, whereas some givers are inclined to give up their souls to avoid rejection or abandonment. Relating styles tend to be handed down from generation to generation, almost like genes. Takers model taking as a way of life but can also encourage their children to be givers, since giving can become a pathway for survival with their taking parent. Likewise, givers may raise up children who will make giving their way of life, or they can inspire their children to become takers, who are accustomed to receiving but not giving. Quite often, children grow up observing one parent tending more to be a giver and one parent more a taker. Without being conscious of it, children absorb the drama of give-and-take with each passing day. Imperceptibly, they are drawn to a style of relating without even choosing it. They are deceived into believing that loving is either getting what you want from others or making sacrifices to give others what they want.

On the face of it, developing a relating style seems to be a matter of learning. There is something deeper going on. Both givers and takers are relating with others in isolation. Even though two people may be physically together, they have the choice to be open with one another or closed. For the most part, givers and takers keep what they want to themselves and figure out how to take care of what they want alone. There is an ever-present expectation that it is unsafe to reveal one's desires, since there seems a high probability that others will either interfere or become angry and rejecting. Connections between givers and takers on a deep level are weak or nonexistent. Life is a shallow commerce in selfishness and selflessness.

In the absence of connection, the only possible way givers and takers can relate is through conditional acceptance and rejection. Takers are very obvious in their use of this weapon; givers more subtly use the weapon against themselves. Takers usually begin by offering what appears to be an unconditional acceptance in order to seduce and win trust. They can appear unusually kind and generous in order to make a good first impression. Once a measure of trust is gained, continued acceptance will be based on conditions: namely, handing over to the taker what he wants. The taker acts as if he is in a position to judge the value, importance, lovability, or capability of others. Takers depend upon others to be fooled into believing their judgments. Takers use rejection, either open or implied, to intimidate or discourage others from pursuing their own desires, and they use it to punish whomever may not be giving them what they want. The shallow preoccupation with moment-to-moment comfort spawns addictions of all sorts, a growing callousness towards others, and/or an amoral way of life. Happiness is impossible. Inner boredom and emptiness inspire a reckless and ruthless search for relief. The soul approaches death.

Givers have abiding doubts about their worth, lovability, and capability. They conditionally accept and reject themselves. Generally they feel worthwhile if they are pleasing others but are filled with guilt and shame if they disappoint. They fear and loathe selfishness. They believe self-sacrifice is a virtue of overriding importance. Givers fear takers, but they will try to defend themselves by giving. Givers can give until there is nothing left to give. They may sacrifice so many desires that they become rundown and get sick. Sometimes after a binge of giving and self-sacrifice, they erupt in a flash of anger, which is followed by waves of guilt that can only be relieved by giving more. They crave loving, yet they fear closeness, because they sense danger. They can't stand being alone but are cautious about getting close, since they are sure rejection will come. They live in a constant state of anxiety and helplessness. They feel abandoned by everyone, even God.

The lives of givers and takers reveal the unmistakable influence of Satan. He isolates. He deceives. He exploits. He perverts true love into a pseudo love that is actually a pernicious and deadly method of hurting. He is determined to destroy whomever God loves and whoever would love God. He attacks love, because God is love and loving is of God. There is no life or instance of loving that is safe from his attacks. He is wiser, more powerful, and infinitely more experienced than any human being. He means to plunge the whole world into darkness.

EIGHT MONTHS after Brit died, Gretchen began her studies in environmental science at the University of Maine at Fort Kent. She was hopeful that a new chapter in her life was about to open. She was taking her first steps outside the realm of expectations that others had for her life. She loved nature, animals, and plants, and she marveled at the beauty, complexity, and mystery of ecosystems.

She also took an elective course in the fine arts department. Early on, the professor asked her students to make a drawing of anything they liked. Self-consciously Gretchen began to draw. The professor walked around the room, looking at the students' work. Before the professor could comment on her work, Gretchen said her drawing was pathetic. The professor asked her when the last time she drew simply for the pleasure of it was. This surprising question gave her pause for thought. She answered, when she was seven years old. With a smile for encouragement the professor told her, "Now you can pick up where you left off."

At a moment when Gretchen was expecting rejection, she was given acceptance. She was stunned. This safety to be herself was unfamiliar. She had never thought she possessed talent. For the first time, she believed it was possible. Over the next three years, she immersed herself in her art. She found a talent and developed it with abandon. She had found a condition to accept herself. Art gave her joy, but it also intensified her insecurity, since beauty is in the eye of the beholder. The more she learned, the more she realized what she didn't know. As she explored different media, she developed basic skills in drawing, composition, painting, photography, woodcuts, collage, and writing. As Gretchen came to appreciate the skills of other artists, she reflexively gave too much importance to what she could not do. Her passion and joy were also a form of torture. As she drove herself to win acceptance as an artist, traumas of loss and rejection were accumulating. Her father, who finally, near the end of his life, managed a loving relationship with her, died of cancer. At midnight, after driving seventeen hours to visit her father's graveside, she drove into oncoming traffic in the Baltimore Tunnel, crashing into a tractor-trailer. Miraculously escaping death, her ankle was crushed beyond repair. Following surgery, it was discovered that she was pregnant. Between the drugs she had been prescribed before the accident and the anesthesia she had been given during the surgery, the pregnancy with her long anticipated first child was compromised.

There would be other car accidents, two other beloved West Highland terriers who would drown in an ice-ringed winter pond, several surgeries, infertility ordeals, sexual harassments and assaults, failed businesses, arrests and accidents while driving intoxicated, battles with addictions to alcohol and drugs, hospitalizations for suicidal intentions, incarcerations, lawsuits, psychiatric disabilities, a marriage being crushed by the weight of it all, and finally, on September 2, 1997, a diagnosis of terminal lung cancer.

Even though I witnessed and accompanied Gretchen in her agonizing descent into darkness, I know I could not begin to understand her suffering. There were many nights when all I could do was hold her in my arms as she was convulsing in unbearable pain. My helplessness was a personal agony. All my life I wanted to love and be loved. My determined hope that loving her would eventually save her grew dimmer with each blow to her being. I was dying with her.

ALTHOUGH THE story of everyone's life is personal and unique, unlike the life of anyone else, every life knows the darkness of rejection. It is the cancer of the soul. Separating, isolating, confining, hurting, frightening; instilling helplessness, mistrust, confusion, conflict, and turmoil; and draining people of their faith, hope, and life, rejection is the perfect solvent for the ruination and elimination of loving relationships. People take it in without even knowing it, becoming increasingly rejecting of themselves, viewing everything that transpires in their relationships through its distorted lens. It feeds on itself and is all consuming. We will give to others what we receive and get back more of what we give. As we sink into rejection's grip, addictions proliferate as we desperately search for comfort alone, further alienating ourselves from others. A true loving relationship is too frightening to enter, for there we will surely be revealed and cast away as unworthy and defiled. Even in relationships that are basically loving from time to time, rejection will rear its ugly head. Whenever importance veers away from the true balance of equality, whenever we are drawn by our nature, the sirens of the world, and Satan himself to care more about ourselves, we walk down the Way of Happiness into darkness, not knowing someone had switched the signs.

In its essence, rejection is sin, and just as yeast completely leavens bread, so too rejection pervades all the dimensions of human relationships. It is active in friendships, anonymous relationships, marriages, families, classrooms and schools, churches, businesses and industry, communities, societies, cultures, economic systems, and political relationships. Ultimately, it is the source of all hurt and evil, as well as destructive conflict and stress, which fuels poverty, violence, injustice, and disease. It is a most powerful, invisible dimension of our reality that most of us do not know is there. It is so obvious we can't see it. It is so pernicious that when it is seen, we can't escape it. It has become woven into our being, imprinted and conditioned into our brains so pervasively; it is a part of our nature as human beings. It is "normal," an accepted and expected feature of living. It is the opposite of loving. It is absolute darkness.

CHAPTER FOUR

The Light

Behold, for peace I had great bitterness: but thou hast in love to my soul delivered it from the pit of corruption: for thou hast cast all my sins behind thy back.

—Isaiah 38:17 (KJV)

BEATEN, BLOODIED, and discouraged, you have retreated once again to the safety of the crossroads. There you contemplate the two miserable choices and your hopelessness. You don't want to go on, but you don't want to stay where you are. You roll over on your back, grateful for the ground that is holding your weight as you look up into the sky. Your body is warmed by the sun. It comes to you for the first time that you have been blessed with the light. Overlooked, taken for granted, a visitor every day, sure and certain, it is there before and after darkness. As you wonder about the source of the light, the Path of Doom is illuminated with a bright, peaceful light that melts your fears and gives you strength to stand. As you step into the shimmering golden light of the path, your doubts disappear and you are filled with the sense for the first time that you are walking in truth. There is a welcoming beauty of gardens on both sides of the path, teeming with wildlife living in harmony together. As you walk in the light down the path, it isn't long before you come upon other people, each of them having come from another crossroads alone, much like yourself. Their faces reflect an abiding joy within them and a rich pleasure that you also feel as you meet. You are astonished by what is unfolding. Your pain, hopelessness, and loneliness have gone. The light has revealed to everyone the wisdom of loving.

As THE snows of winter melt into spring, the blueberry fields are warmed and generously drink the water of life. The roots of the vines send up leaf buds that unfold in the sun, collecting energy for growth. From the charred, desolate fields come sweeping waves of green, glistening in the soft breezes and sunlight. A multitude of delicate white blueberry flower bells bloom on the vines of plants scorched by the mechanical burners eighteen months ago. The plants are determined to see life go on in even greater abundance. Bumblebees, native bees, and honeybees visit the bells, looking for nectar, spreading pollen from plant to plant, and enabling the conception of a remarkably rich fruit that can help prevent cancer and Alzheimer's disease. My family and I gratefully labor in the fields to undo what people possessed of greed had taken, and we give back to God the care of His creation.

ON THE third day after the crucifixion of Christ, Mary Magdalene; Mary, the mother of James; Joanna; and other women went to the tomb where the body of Jesus was laid. They found the stone rolled away from the tomb and the body of Jesus gone. Two angels were there and told them, "Why do you seek the living among the dead? He spoke to you when he was still in Galilee, saying, 'The Son of Man must be delivered into the hands of sinful men, and be crucified, and the third day rise again'" Luke 24:5–7(NKJV).

The greatest of all prophecies had been fulfilled. The dream of humankind to be freed from evil and themselves had come true. God's love had prevailed over rejection and death. The Father's love for us, despite our sin, weakness, and limitations was so extraordinary; He humbled Himself and became one of us, lived a perfectly loving life, then gave His life for us so that we could be with Him forever. He understands our helpless predicament and the magnitude of the forces arrayed against us. He was moved with passion to come for us, step into the breach and save us, protect us, guide our way through life, and love us inspirationally into eternity.

Gretchen told me about her cancer diagnosis as I drove her home from the hospital, after treatment was started for pneumonia. I was shocked, disoriented, and confused; my body was numb, breathless. A feeling of unreality swept over me. Deep waves of gut-wrenching sadness erupted. Time stood still while I held her hand, and we looked into each other's tear-filled eyes, not saying a word. When I took her hand, I felt a deep joining of our spirits that I had never felt before. It was as if we had sailed through a violent storm and passed into calm waters. We were of one mind and one heart. Most miraculous of all, the hurt of Gretchen's lifetime was gone, and she was completely open and welcoming of love. She told me she was determined to fight for her life, even though as a nurse, she knew the cancer had advanced to a late stage.

Together, we set out to learn as much as we could about her cancer, as well as both the traditional and alternative treatments that were in practice around the world. We conferred with a variety of doctors, obtained other medical opinions, had a consultation at Dana-Farber Hospital in Boston, and with the help of friends, even managed to obtain medicines that were not available in the United States. One treatment involved the use of "Coley's Toxin," an agent which took the body through a roller coaster of body temperature: first she experienced an extremely high fever, which potentially could weaken the tumor; that was followed by a sudden drop in core body temperature, producing violent shivering and chills, which could only be buffered with many layers of blankets. Bravely, Gretchen went through this personal treatment several times, a hellish ride through extreme body discomfort that lasted several hours. She took a variety of supplements to boost her immune system, which already had been compromised by pneumonia. In fact, because of her pneumonia, traditional strategies to attack the tumor had to be postponed. Due to the location of the tumor, surgery was not an option. The pneumonia was stealing what little hope there was and allowing the cancer to progress freely.

Independent of each other, Gretchen and I sought Jesus. While we had both considered ourselves Christians, we had lived as if Jesus were absent from our day-to-day lives for thirty years. We did not pray, read the Bible, or attend church, other than an occasional holiday service. Now, we were asking Him to save her life. We were asking Him to be with our twin sons, Galen and Christian, and with us; we were asking Him to comfort us, and love us. We were overwhelmed. He was our only hope.

Jesus more than answered our prayers, although not in the way we had expected. Loving erupted in full brilliance in our family. It seemed like every day and moment He was with us. Every glance, smile, touch, and act between us and our children overflowed with love. Everything else disappeared. There was extraordinary clarity about what was important and what was not. Fears and doubts were gone. We were at peace. Jesus was carrying all of us with Him to the end of Gretchen's life and to the beginning of eternity with Him. Gently yet profoundly, He was preparing my sons and me to live loving lives with Him and others forever. I remember how peculiar it was to be living out such an incredible love at a time when I would have thought fear and sadness would have been ruling our day-to-day lives. However, nothing could have been further from the truth.

About a month after Gretchen was diagnosed, she met with the remarkably loving and faithful Christian woman who had taken care of our children after school for several years and who had become a trusted and caring friend. Her name was Theresa Hileman. Together, they prayed, and Gretchen gave her life completely to Jesus. Deep in prayer, Gretchen entered into Jesus' presence. His love and peace filled her. His mercy forgave and cleansed her. He restored and expanded exponentially her faith and hope. Theresa and Gretchen prayed together, tearfully and joyfully, in a most healing emotional and spiritual experience. Jesus did not heal her body; however He went infinitely beyond our prayers and sealed a loving relationship with Gretchen, our children, and me, forever.

This was an experience for our family that in some ways must have been like the experience of Moses as he stepped into the presence of God at the burning bush. "And the Lord said: 'I have surely seen the oppression of my people, who are in Egypt, and have heard their cry, because of their taskmasters, for I know their sorrows. So, I have come down to deliver them out of the hand of the Egyptians, and to bring them up from that land to a good and large land, to a land flowing with milk and honey'" Exodus 3:7–8(NKJV).

We were fortified and equipped before the monsters of pain and cancer came to ravage and destroy Gretchen's body. The disease advanced like a refiner's fire, melting away the debris and impurities of our lives, leaving only a pure, solid core of loving. When she died, she went from my arms to the arms of Jesus. In return, He gave me a mission, together with the Holy Spirit, to be a witness and a disciple of His love for all.

IN THE beginning, God created the heavens and the earth. He created the stage on which the drama of His love for us would unfold (Genesis 1:1). He filled the stage with light (Genesis 1:3). He formed the land and the oceans (Genesis 1:6, 9). He seeded the land with beautiful varieties of flowers, trees, and fruits for the protection, nurturing, and enjoyment of His beloved children (Genesis 1:11). He created the dimension of time for days and nights and seasons and years in which His children could grow, love, play, and work with Him (Genesis 1:14). He gave life to the creatures of the sea, birds to fly over the earth, and creatures to live on the land to delight, inspire, serve, and help His children (Genesis1:20, 24). Lastly, He created, in His own image, man and woman for the simple and complete purpose of loving Him and each other (Genesis 1:25, 27).

God's creations reveal His glory, endless greatness, and amazing love. Each human life is one of His miracles. It is unlikely science will ever understand the nature of life and existence. It may map the genetic code and describe the combination of molecules that make up DNA. Science may tell us about the behavior and structure of atoms and the relatively vast "empty space" contained in each one, but the essence of life and existence shall elude the observations of science, because this is beyond the realm of observation. This is the grandest dimension of being created in His image: our spiritual essence. As people living in a "physical and social reality," it is difficult to comprehend or imagine that the most important dimension of our being is spiritual. What is concrete and right in front of our eyes; what can be touched, experienced, and acted on; and even what is beyond us in our immediate and distant environments all have the appearance of what is real. Each experience or perceived reality that goes on inside of us (our sensations, perceptions, learning and memories, thoughts and beliefs, imaginings, emotions, moral judgments, hopes, dreams, desires and plans, language and communication, understanding of others, and projections of ourselves) is the manifestation of countless neural synapses orchestrated symphonically in our brains; these manifestations are assumed to be real and true without our being aware of it. Yet, looking at the history of human experience, society, culture, politics, economics, and science, it is apparent that what appears to be real is actually quite arbitrary.

The human body is made up of over one hundred trillion cells. It is an interesting metaphor for the earth or even the universe: one hundred trillion parts, each with a purpose or contribution to the working of the whole, organized and acting according to a fixed set of rules, interdependent, directly and indirectly collaborating with all the other parts. These parts are fluid, adaptable, dynamic, changing and learning with change and challenge; the workings of the body are as mysterious as God Himself. The human body is awesome to behold in its beauty, complexity, efficiency, and economy; yet, it is only a hint of the limitless grandeur of its Creator. Each of us has one: a priceless vessel containing the gift of life, making possible sensing, creating, thinking, feeling, acting, growth, learning, problem-solving, communicating, relating and loving, the operations of mind and heart. It can protect us from foreign invaders and enemies both microscopic and "life-size." It can heal itself in many different ways. It possesses an extraordinary wisdom for doing what it does without our even having to think about it: consuming, digesting, and absorbing food and drink, distributing nutrients and oxygen to each cell while removing wastes, communicating and governing the activity among all the parts by way of millions of chemical, hormonal, and electrical messages simultaneously. What an extraordinary gift to give to someone who is loved!

The human brain is considered to be so complex that human beings will never be able to understand how it works, and yet, we can hold it in the palms of our hands. Its collective capacities far exceed the operation of the most sophisticated network of computers and will likely always remain so. It is the organ of the mind, heart, and spirit, reflecting on an infinitely modest scale, corresponding dimensions of God. Most of its activity occurs automatically without conscious direction. It gathers, sorts, and interprets a wealth of information sampled from the environment and from the body itself. In a split second, information is processed in the light of previous experience or memory, forming an understanding that can be used as the basis of a formulation for responding. The flow of consciousness is like a river containing perceptions, memories, thoughts, emotions, desires, intuition, and ideas for action, impulses, values, and moral judgments. Overseeing it all is, perhaps, the most remarkable of the mind's gifts: the ability to exercise choice, or free will.

At any given moment, we are free to choose how we will live and act in that moment. Perhaps most of the time, we do not exercise this free will but rather coast along on "automatic pilot"; in other words, we live out of our habits, which were established through past experience. Our habits can be a blessing or a curse. Surely, they simplify the countless tasks of living; however, we can become captive to our habits, endlessly repeating what may not be working very well. Addictions, in particular, may carry a person down a real Path of Doom to her death. With our freedom of choice, we can interrupt habits, reflect on our moment-to-moment experience, and change how we think, feel, act, or communicate with others. With our free will, we can deliberately practice and build new habits. We can shift what we believe. We can learn from past mistakes and form a vision of how we would like to live, and then pursue it.

How we act depends greatly upon how we think, or what we believe. Having a mind that can believe and that has free will begs the following questions: What shall we believe? How did we become believers? What is the purpose of believing? These questions might be addressed in a shallow way, simply by claiming it is the nature of human beings; it is a function resulting from neurological structures that have evolved from the beginning of time, serving the purpose of human survival. This view denies the spiritual dimension of our being, diminishes our value, and makes our purpose somewhat arbitrary. If we are honest with ourselves intuitively, we will admit there is something missing in these answers.

Profound answers flow when we contemplate these questions from a spiritual perspective. The incredible complexity, beauty, and order of the human body, mind, soul, and life itself could neither be the result of countless chance accidents or mutations; they could only be the work of a Grand Designer who created us for loving relationships with Him and each other. We can believe because it was His plan that we would believe in Him. We believe so that we can maintain a connection with Him. We believe so that we can communicate with Him and grow in a loving relationship with Him that would give purpose and meaning to our lives and our relationships with others. Without the ability to believe, loving would be impossible. Survival is only the beginning of the story; loving is the end. We were made for loving, because loving is His essence, and we are the objects of His love. How grandly we are elevated by His love, how noble is our purpose, and how glorious is our God!

By the time our nervous systems mature, questions arise about what exactly we will believe, and they continue throughout our lives. In our maturity, we are able to reflect and choose what we will believe. Yet, it can be so subtle at times, we do not realize we are choosing what to believe. We exist, are alive, can sense, think, choose, and act, because a miracle has occurred. We had nothing to do with the miracle. Sure, we could say it was a miracle of union between egg and sperm, but what was the origin of sperm and eggs? How did they come to be? How did genetic material, DNA and basic proteins, come to be? It was a miracle of creation. So, in what or in whom shall we believe? In the creation or the Creator? It would behoove us to choose carefully, because the consequences of our choice are as starkly different as darkness and light.

Realizing the foibles of our ability to believe, we must also be careful to choose the true God. There are well over one hundred religions practiced presently on Earth, not including esoteric spirituality and personally devised beliefs or philosophies. Clearly, there is a great yearning in human beings for spiritual communion with God. We are apt to squander our belief on gods of our own, or human beings' creation, as opposed to the God of our creation. Chuck Smith of Calvary Chapel Ministries has observed that there is only one religion where God has actively sought out a relationship with humankind, as opposed to humankind seeking out a relationship with God. There is only one religion where God has become a human being in a daring and bold act of love, to secure a relationship between humankind and God. There is only one religion where God inspired a multitude of authors spanning thousands of years to write a book containing His wisdom, truth, and love to illuminate the past, present, and future. Only one faith is validated by the fulfillment of hundreds of specific prophecies, most notably that Jesus Christ, both God and man, would be the Savior of the world. He would be humbly born, live a perfectly loving life, reveal all essential truths in His miraculous teaching ministry, give His own life in order to save humankind, rise from the dead in glory, and ascend into heaven. It is a religion whose only purpose is to support believers' loving relationship with the true God. The religion is Christianity.

God has not specifically defined love in the Bible. Yet, the Bible in its essence is a love story. God has revealed that He is love. Perhaps there is no definition, because just as God is infinite and beyond our ability to grasp, so too is His love. Defining love would limit it. If we look at the thousands of verses in the Bible where the word *love* or *loving* appears, we are provided some clues about the profound and robust nature of God's love. His love is honest and true, forgiving and merciful, full of grace and peace, righteous, just and fair, protective and strong, rebuking, correcting, guiding, kind and giving, helpful and hopeful, patient and long-suffering, persistent and enduring, promise keeping, good and gentle, slow to anger, compassionate and empathetic, sincere, loyal, encouraging, joyful, and friendly. God's love provides us with the ultimate model of loving for our own relationships. His love is active, dynamic, and dramatic. It is so much more than a tender feeling or bond. When we act in accordance with His design for loving, we experience happiness in its purest form. When we stray from its profound wisdom, we shall have no peace. His love is powerfully inviting and relentlessly pursuing. He loves us and wants our love for our own good—not out of a need that He has, but rather because it is part of His nature. His love is the light of the world.

CHAPTER FIVE

Going Back for the Lost

For the Son of Man is come to save that which was lost.

—Matthew 18:11 (KJV)

PEOPLE OF all ages have gathered in the light on the true Way of Happiness. There is peace and joy in their eyes. Their smiles are welcoming. Each has adventures in loving to share with passion and excitement. The people are overflowing with gratitude for their happiness. They have never felt so safe, complete, or content. The air they breathe and the light surrounding them are bright, clear, and pure. The path is bordered by an amazing variety of beautiful flowers, their colors soft but radiant in the light. Beyond the flowers are groves of plump, delicious fruit trees: apple, pear, peach, orange, cherry, kiwi, and others that aren't even recognizable. They are nestled together without seeming out of place. Animals and birds of wondrous diversity play, rest, and forage together in the fields and forests that stretch off into the distance. It is joyful and delightful to behold their unique beauty and character. Off in the distance there are other paths that seem to come from all directions, winding their way to a point on the horizon that glows brilliantly and intensely with the same light that seems to fill everyone on the path with love. Most astonishing of all are the people. Each has an amazing beauty all his own. Beyond the dazzle of the most precious jewels or the gentle brilliance of the rising sun, their faces glow with a simple and profound kindness. They greet each other with respect and reverence that is warm and genuine. They are irresistibly drawn to know and care for one another. They listen with openness, stillness, and awe. They appreciate listening as if it were the simultaneous giving and receiving of a valuable gift. Listening seems like a spirited dance performed as one, drawing them ever more deeply into a common peace. Truth is spoken by all as if it were the only language they ever knew. Each word is an act of love, offered deliberately in gratitude and humility. Each person is as pleased to share her unique gifts and beauty as she is to enjoy and celebrate the treasure of others' hearts and spirits. Stories, songs, and laughter abound as the people embrace, play, and give thanks for the love and the light about them. You all remember vividly being at the crossroads, before you found the light. You have a powerful desire to continue on the path, to follow it to its end, but first, you all agree you will go back to the crossroads to show others the light.

ANYONE FAMILIAR with the blueberry business in Maine knows it is a dirty business, driven by greed. Recently, a class-action suit was brought by over five hundred blueberry growers against three of the largest processing plants and brokers of wild Maine blueberries. A jury found the processors guilty of fixing and depressing the prices paid to the growers for their fruit. The judgment, if it stands could bankrupt the processors, leaving the growers with scarce resources to care for their fields and nowhere to sell their fruit. At harvest time, crew bosses assemble gangs of generally poor, seasonal, and migrant workers, as well as school-age youth looking for summer work, to do the hard labor of raking the fields. The bosses take a percentage of what is raked and skim off the top any excess of twenty pounds, the standard measure for a box of blueberries. It is a common practice for the bosses to insist that the rakers make sure their boxes have more than twenty pounds. The economy and the politics of the business encourage lying, cheating, and stealing. It has grown increasingly difficult for the bosses to find enough laborers to bring in the harvest. Greed has reached the point of diminishing returns.

As stewards of twenty-two acres of wild Maine blueberries, our family decided years ago to grow organically and to seek out people of all ages who believed and loved Jesus Christ to join us in caring for the fields, harvesting the crop, and bringing it to market. Each day of work begins with prayer and thanks. The work is a labor of love for all. When other growers lost their crop to drought or could not afford to harvest because of depressed field prices, the

Lord blessed us with abundance, prosperity, and joy! Now we are looking for other growers to join us.

NOT LONG after Gretchen was diagnosed, and her faith in Christ was sealed, we received the news that my six-year-old niece, Annie, had been diagnosed with two rare forms of deadly brain cancer. For some time leading up to the diagnosis, Annie had been having spells of raging moods and wild behavior. She was growing more and more withdrawn from her family. Conflict between her parents also grew as they struggled to cope and understand. When her diagnoses had been made, it was like an explosion in her family. A cauldron of anger, grief, and fear was poured out on her family. Annie could not understand what was happening, but she knew she was sick, and she knew what was happening around her was because of it. Her spirit was beginning to die.

We lived five hundred miles away from Annie, so it was impractical to visit; however, on a beautiful Sunday afternoon in the fall, Gretchen called Annie. They would have a miraculous conversation. Having their sickness and the prospect of death in common, this woman and child shared capacities for understanding that were unique. Bravely together, they vowed to fight for their lives and help each other to face what was coming with faith and love. Fourteen years later, Annie has survived and bravely lives on.

Seamlessly, loving flowed on as Gretchen passed away. We cleansed and anointed her body, combed and brushed her hair, modestly made up her face with her own cosmetics, dressed her beautifully and adorned her with her favorite jewelry. We placed her in an open casket in our sunroom, surrounded by her flowers and the art of her life. Family and friends gathered informally over several days, sharing their love with ours. For grieving, honoring, and sharing our amazing discovery of loving, I matted and framed over one hundred works of her art—paintings, photographs, and collages—for a month-long show and celebration of her life. As the years have gone by, many of her works have been given to people we have loved, along with this remarkable story.

STEPPING OUT of the darkness and into the profound light of God's love is truly like being born again. There is clarity about what is real and what is not, what is important and what is unimportant, what is truth, what is joy, what is peace, and what is the meaning and purpose of life. Finally, everything makes sense. This experience is powerfully moving. The only thing that makes sense to do next is to share it with as many people as possible. A loving relationship with God is the essential driving force of true loving with others. Without it, there will always be a sense that something is missing, incomplete, and finite. The depth of loving will be limited. The vulnerability to insecurity, self-absorption, confusion, conflict, disappointment, hurt, and rejection will be relentless.

Since God is love and He gave us life for the sake of a loving relationship with Him, it would be wise to consider how He loves us, so that we might love others as He loves us. As anyone who is living in a loving relationship with God can attest, the Bible directly or indirectly speaks to us about the nature of God's loving in every book, in every chapter, and in every verse. In the gospel of John, we are privileged to view the portrait of loving in the life of the true master, Jesus Christ. Inspired by the Holy Spirit, John reveals brilliantly pure and perfect loving in the words and deeds of Jesus.

The Unmerited Favor of Grace— Unconditional Acceptance

> And of His fullness have all we received, and grace for grace. John 1:16 (KJV)

The fullness and profound nature of the relationship between the Father, Jesus, and the Holy Spirit is beyond our comprehension. Yet, they have made obvious by words and deeds all the essential ingredients for perfect loving. The foundation from which all the other ingredients flow is an unconditional acceptance. In the Trinity, this attribute of relationship is perfectly actualized; the Father, Jesus, and the Holy Spirit are one. Each member of the Godhead has a unique role and identity. Yet, so sweeping and complete is their acceptance of each other that their interest in knowing and believing in each other, their willingness to give their all to each other, and their pleasure and joy in serving each other are all infinite. Unconditional acceptance is at the core of God's love and nature. It is the binding of their connection with one another. It is at the heart of God's relationship with us. In spite of our endless limitations, selfishness, disinterest, rejection, conditional acceptance, and forgetfulness of Him, He is steadfastly open, interested, pursuing, forgiving, welcoming, and accepting of us to the moment of our death. This favor, which is so unmerited, is the grace of God. He is seeking and, by the Holy Spirit, leading us into an unconditional acceptance of Him as our Father God. He wants us to belong to Him, believe in Him, trust in Him, come to know Him, and give our all for Him, for the sake of being perfectly loved, at peace, and in joy from now to eternity. Nothing else can come close to living this well.

Jesus refers to the radiant unconditional acceptance of God for Him and for us in John 3:16: "For God so loved the world that He gave his one and only Son, that whoever believes in Him shall not perish but have eternal life." God is willing to give absolutely everything that matters to Him to secure a relationship with us. His acceptance of us is as unconditional as His acceptance of His Son. No less an authority than Jesus delivers the Father's invitation to us to believe and unconditionally accept the Father and His great love for us. The Father and Jesus, furthermore, provide a model for how we may practice unconditional acceptance in our relationships with Jesus and others. Jesus believes in His Father, accepts and trusts Him, does what His Father asks without question, joining the Father in mutual love. The Father treasures Jesus above Himself and asks us to believe in Him as He does, giving importance to a loving relationship with Jesus, as He does, and to the acts of loving themselves for His glory and our well-being as His beloved children.

A true miracle occurs when we live in an unconditional acceptance of God, when we believe in Him. When grace meets faith, from that moment on, we are safe and secure. All the trials, challenges, problems, and troubles we may face in this life will be small stuff. On a moment-to-moment basis, God is with us, and we are with Him. He will protect us from the ever-present forces of evil. He will overshadow the temptations of the world, and He will free us from the solitary confinement of our selfishness. We will be able to see, as if for the first time, the truth stripped of all deception. We will know what is important and what is not. We will know our place in the world, our reason for being, and our purpose, without any doubts. The meaning of life will be clear, pure, and simple. We will be immune from the rejection of others and filled with compassion for those living in the darkness. We will be healed of all hurts suffered in our journeys through life. We will understand what loving is all about and be ready to joyously practice it as a lifestyle. We will be prepared to graciously insist that everyone we know join us in mutual, unconditionally accepting relationships. And best of all, after our momentary lifetimes, we shall live forever in a loving relationship with God and all those who love Him.

> Then they asked him, "What must we do to do the works God requires?" Jesus answered, "The work of God is this: to believe in the one he has sent." John 6:28–29(NIV2011)

Unconditional acceptance requires us to believe in Jesus, which requires us to follow the example of His life. The belief that Jesus is talking about is not something that is conceptual or limited to a feeling in our hearts. True belief demands we back it up with action. Belief is measured by what we do. Every act in the life of Jesus was an expression of His unconditional acceptance of His Father and of us. He did exactly what His Father asked Him to do—no more, no less. He set aside His own ideas and His own will and riveted His complete attention on what His Father wanted. He was leading us by His example. He was showing us the way through the hell of living to the safe passage of loving.

Our first priority is our own unique relationship with God, because without it we can do nothing; without it we are lost. Just as Jesus did, we must give our complete attention to what God wants of us, setting aside our own desires. We must do what God wants, trusting that He knows far better than we do how to live and love, and trusting that what He wants for us is infinitely better than what we might want for ourselves. God wants us to love Him and others, every moment, with all our beings.

When we are grounded in an unconditionally accepting way of life with God, then and only then are we ready to live in an unconditionally accepting way with others. Without this basic bond with God, we are profoundly alone, even in the midst of busy and full social lives. No one will ever visit our own minds and hearts. At best, we can tell others what we think and feel, but they cannot know it as we do, or as God does. We can touch another's face, look into another's eyes, but we can never join him inside as God can. In our aloneness we give excessive importance to ourselves, assume justification for scheming to obtain what we want from others, and unwittingly sow the seeds for emptiness, boredom, and conflict in our relationships with others. Without an unconditionally loving relationship with God, our values ultimately will be self-serving. When we can obtain from God all the necessities of loving, we then are free, comfortable, patient, and capable to develop loving relationships with others based on the same values of our relationship with God.

> All that the Father gives me will come to me, and whoever comes to me, I will never drive away.
> John 6:37

The acceptance of Jesus is so complete: He is alert, open, available, and actively and thoroughly gathering all that His Father gives to Him. He does not want to miss anything. To do this requires an amazing selflessness. Jesus deliberately sets aside His own desires in order to maximize His awareness of His Father's desires. He welcomes and accepts His Father's presence, attention, words, ideas, thoughts, feelings, values, desires, will, support, and love. Surely, the Father accepted Jesus in the same way. Accepting Jesus on these terms is what coming to Him is all about. Jesus tells us anyone who accepts Him completely will be accepted completely and never rejected by God. Imagine how glorious your life would be if you could accept all that Jesus could give!

Now imagine what would happen if you accepted others unconditionally and were likewise accepted by others. At first blush, this might seem like a risky, foolhardy, and naïve way to relate with others. After all, it is fairly uncommon to find people who would accept us without condition, and we all have known people who were untrustworthy, manipulative, and selfish. Such people don't announce their intentions beforehand. They may be practiced in the arts of deception or seduction. Truth be told, haven't we all acted this way at one time or another? Notice, however, how Jesus handles these problems. He insists we accept Him first, before He gives His grand gifts. He is ready to bless us with so much more than His acceptance, His grace, which He freely offers. He certainly is inviting us to accept Him; however, He patiently waits to see what we are going to do, how we will exercise our choice. Will we truly come to Him, or will we place a higher value on what we desire? Jesus will join us if we will join Him. He will not drive us away if we do not join Him. He simply allows us to have what we want, along with its miserable consequences of being alone, without Him. He doesn't help us obtain what we want, nor does He spare us the consequences. He is remarkably accepting, even when we're off track. He does not withdraw His offer of acceptance, no matter how we act, and He is ready to extend forgiveness if we seek it with our hearts and give Him what He desires, acceptance.

Insisting on mutual, unconditional acceptance in our relationships with others is a formidable shield and protection from people who would accept us conditionally, reject us, use us, or abuse us. Insisting continually, on a moment-to-moment basis, in unconditional acceptance in all relationships will insure that the lost and selfish will get nowhere trying to get what they want. They will be given a choice to continue their solitary pursuit of selfish desires or join with you in mutual acceptance and collaboration. Only one way will work; all others will fail. Those who are willing to join you will begin developing a loving relationship with you. Those who don't will be alone by their choice. As time goes on, your life will be filled more and more with mutually accepting and loving relationships.

Insisting on mutual acceptance will lead and guide others into loving experiences. Sadly, most people are living defensively in their relationships, either selfishly concerning themselves with getting what they want or selflessly caring more about pleasing others so they will not be hurt or rejected. When we require mutual acceptance, we are offering a lifesaving gift, a critical ingredient for successful loving in all relationships. We are inviting others to experience a new way of living that is fuller, more meaningful, and more joyous than anything they have known before. We may give them practice in crucial skills that may eventually become habits for loving deeply. Thus, we can invite them to share in the healing love of God.

Each of us is one of a kind. We are unique, genetically and experientially. There never has been, nor will there ever be, anyone just like any of us. Truly, no one has ever seen exactly what our eyes have seen, nor heard what our ears have heard, nor shared a moment of our own mental awareness. Our unique experiences are stored only in our own brains, forming the raw data for our opinions, ideas, perceptions, thoughts, beliefs, emotions, hopes, dreams, and schemes for acting in the world, as well as for relating with others. If we are going to change anything, it will be our own doing. Therefore, when anyone tampers with us in any way, instantly we will become defensive and resist. When we are given unconditional acceptance, we perceive conditions of safety, peace, and trust, which are all requisites for any meaningful interaction.

Primarily, we have fear, born out of past experiences, that we will not be able to have what we want if we give unconditional acceptance to others. These experiences were no doubt valid when we were interacting with conditionally accepting and rejecting people who were concerned only with how they could obtain what they wanted. As children, even if we could insist upon unconditional acceptance, which we naturally were yearning, there wasn't much we could do to change older, more powerful people who were prepared to brush aside anything short of getting what they wanted as easily and quickly as possible. As children, we are all taught that life is unfair and that unconditionally accepting others is often associated with hurt. The world is so full of people who are hurtful that the people who insist on mutual acceptance are often considered naïve. Yet, who among us truly has given up hope of finding it? It is our absolute uniqueness as the children of God that establishes our right to receive unconditional acceptance and our responsibility to give it to others. Truly, nothing else makes sense.

> You judge by human standards; I pass judgment
> on no one. John 8:15

Perhaps it goes without saying that when we are unconditionally accepting, judgments are set aside. But, this is easier said than done. It is our nature, it has been our cultural conditioning, it has been our experience in relationships, and it has been a deep spiritual deception to judge others based upon how well they give us what we desire. As children, we are apt to squeal with delight, "Ooooh! I love you, Mommy!" when receiving a gift we longed for. Mother's giving is taken as a measure of love, and the child believes the gift is proof that she is important to her mother. The mother might also get the idea that she is loved by her child and is a good mother because she gives gifts her child enjoys. The reverse may also be true in the eyes of both the child and mother when the child in a mope says, "You don't love me anymore!" after the mother says no to her child's desires.

As teenagers swept up in the process of identity formation, acceptance by peers may become more important than anything. This need fuels the often-destructive process of peer pressure. It is a need that cannot be satisfied. There can never be enough acceptance. Doubts, insecurity, and anxiety are securely bound together with the need for acceptance. Satisfaction of the need is beyond the control of the one in need, and therefore, a measure of desperate helplessness stirs in the soul. There can also be moments of giddy highs for young people when they are given a portion of acceptance. Briefly, they may feel they are important and they matter; their anxieties ebb. But it doesn't last for long, and their search for acceptance resumes.

In the whirlwind of daily life, adults face endless pressure to meet moment-to-moment demands with limited resources of time, energy, and money. It is the rule rather than the exception that adults clash and conflict with each other as each seeks to address his agenda of desires. How easy it is for us to judge those who are in our way, to be annoyed, frustrated, or angry because they don't understand, don't care, or are only thinking about themselves. These judgments seem to happen automatically and spontaneously without any deliberation. Actually, we grew up immersed in a sea of judgment and learned to practice it as we were learning to walk and talk. It is a powerful habit that afflicts everyone. The only way to stop it is to deliberately practice, moment-by-moment, unconditional acceptance.

Jesus was making a profound observation about us when He said we judge by human standards. We are immersed in our humanness, in our world, and in our lives. It is not easy for us to glimpse into the spiritual realm and consider how God may view us. It is not easy to consider other possible ways we have to view others and ourselves. We must step outside the box. Jesus, on the other hand, by His nature, accepts us unconditionally. His judgments, which are about our choices to accept Him and live with Him, are deliberate and right, because He makes them with the Father. Since these choices are made by each of us, involving our own relationship with God, it is none of our business to pass judgment on others ever! Our unconditional acceptance of others is a spiritual lifeline; having been saved by Jesus, we cast the line out to others to call their attention to Him.

> I am the good Shepherd; I know my sheep, and
> my sheep know me—just as the Father knows
> me and I know the Father -- and I lay down my
> life for the sheep. John 10:14-15

Getting to know someone with an attitude of unconditional acceptance is a remarkable journey of discovery. Assumptions, presuppositions, and prejudice are completely abandoned. We feel an unbiased openness to experience others as they are. Each one of us is a profound work of art by God. Each one of us has a unique story and life. The only way we can come to know someone is through unconditional acceptance; otherwise, we distort and contaminate our knowledge of others with our own selfish projections. How we treat others says so much more about us than it does about others. Knowing requires caretaking of the bond between people, establishing trust to encourage openness and truth, faith and patience for the story to be told in one's own voice, and an active devotion to learn and appreciate the teacher. The simple act of moment-to-moment acceptance accomplishes all of this. The complicated part is not doing anything else.

Coming to know the Good Shepherd has been complicated by our nature, our culture, and the dark spiritual forces. The path between not knowing Jesus and knowing Him is cluttered with ignorance, misinformation, unwarranted fear, confusion, perverse social condemnation, flat-out lies, and evil. Many are stuck in their tracks by the conditional acceptance and rejection of people they know, whose judgments they fear. The blind lead the blind. It is difficult to unconditionally accept if one has never known unconditional acceptance. So, Jesus counts on those who do know Him to go out into the world and give to others what He has given to them: the purest love they will ever know. Jesus goes with His sheep, protecting, guiding, supplying, and joyously celebrating the saving of each lost sheep. His acceptance is so deep and complete for His sheep, lost or found, that He has literally laid down His life for them. How great an assurance that He is the way, the truth, and the light. With Him, we will have the power, the courage, and the heart to accept others without condition and to truly know and be known as loving children of God.

Jesus was the first to come back for the lost. Once you know and love Jesus, loving becomes your reason for being. Nothing will stop you from giving this treasure of treasures to everyone you can. Gretchen died in my arms shortly before dawn in early December as she lay in our bed. Jesus had come for her, and for me. With my tears I said, "I will love you forever," as her spirit was freed. Her peace with Jesus filled our sons, our home, and me. I went downstairs, got on my knees before the hearth, and made a fire to warm the house. Right there, I could see clearly how I would live the rest of my life.

CHAPTER SIX

The Grand Illusion

The intensist light of reason and revelation combined cannot shed such blazoning upon the deeper truths in man, as will sometimes proceed from his profoundest gloom.

—Herman Melville from *Pierre: or, the Ambiguities*

THE WALK back to the crossroads is ripe with contradictions. The joy of the light and beauty all around is there, interspersed with the memory of desperate fears. Time seems to be passing slowly and quickly at the same time. You have moments in thought that seem like hours, even while swiftly passing familiar landmarks on the path. You feel new and pure, as if you have lost everything but your essence; yet, each step sparks

74

pictures in your mind of the person you used to be, which now seems unreal. As a child, you had come to believe you were not very lovable and that other people were much more important than you. As a teenager, you desperately wanted to be liked by others and were afraid you would not fit in with the other youth, who were more popular. As a young adult, you were intimidated by the capability and competitiveness of the people who surrounded you. You felt you were a pretender and that even the person you loved would sooner or later see through you. These and other memories come to you as you return to the crossroads.

As you walk in the light, you have the feeling that your body and mind are absorbing it. Oddly, you feel as if you are breathing the light and that somehow its essence is transported by way of the blood throughout your whole body, performing a cleansing and healing. It seems the light is not only seen but actually penetrates your eyes and flows through the optic nerve to bathe your brain in its soothing peace. One by one, the disturbing memories of your past drop like pebbles in a pond of peace. Indeed, the memories fall like rocks to the bottom of your mind, no longer troubling, no longer believed, only a reminder of who you used to be before you found the light.

SPRING COMES slowly to the wild blueberry fields in Maine. Winter lingers and reluctantly surrenders its cold grip. In mid-April, the ground can still be frozen, with the blueberries of the coming summer sleeping in the promise of the vines' roots. Waiting in patience and determination are the hearts of countless other plants. As the sun warms their beds, they will all spring to life. As stewards of the fields, our family readies plans to serve the blueberries a banquet of nutrients, while mounting a selective assault on the weeds that seek the ground, light, and water for their own use.

Commercial growers of blueberries aspire to eliminate everything but blueberry plants by using various herbicides and by shifting the pH of the soil. All the costs of spreading poison on the fields to kill the weeds are difficult to know. Unintended consequences fall like dominoes in the ecosystem. For one thing, natural pollinators are sacrificed with this battle strategy. Growers must import boxes and boxes of honey beehives to pollinate the blueberry flowers. Honeybees, which do not naturally inhabit blueberry fields, will stay in the hives on rainy and many overcast days; thus, fewer plants are pollinated and fewer blueberries will grow.

For the organic grower of blueberries, some weeds are friends and some are foes. There are "weeds" that attract and sustain natural pollinators, such as bumblebees, through the spring and summer. Bumblebees work hard and never take a day off, no matter what the weather. They more vigorously pollinate the blueberry flowers, producing more robust fruit. Other "weeds" provide the ripening blueberries respite from burning summer sun and help gather morning dew to temper the blueberries' thirst during the usual summer drought. Still other "weeds" may offer shelter or food for insects that can control the few insects that would like to feed on the blueberries. We are constantly learning how to tell the difference between the weeds that are our friends and the weeds that are our foes. We have become increasingly deliberate about the weeds we will remove and how. We labor to undo what we and our predecessors had previously done to the fields in the quest to produce as many blueberries as possible.

ONE EARLY summer day I came home from work and found Gretchen collapsed in a chair in our family room with a distinctly disgusted look on her face. Christian was quietly playing with some toys on the floor. When I entered the room, she gave me a cold stare and said bluntly, "Your son is upstairs, and he has been a real pill." Seeing she was drained of energy yet brimming with a muted anger, without saying a word, I turned and went up the stairs to Galen's bedroom. At the top of the stairs, there was a long hallway that went to his room. His door was closed and, I presumed, locked. I walked down the hall with an easy, gentle gait. I knew he could hear me coming. When I reached his door, I stopped, paused a moment, and lightly knocked. Instantly my eight-year-old son screamed for me to go away and leave him alone. He cried out in pain, "I hate you!" I sat down by his door to accept him with all that he was feeling, to let my silence absorb his rejection.

Since Galen could hear that I did not go away, I believed his silence was asking me to stay. After a couple of minutes, I lightly tapped on his door again. He let out another rejecting howl, a pained cry that seemed to say that he was hurting more than he could bear and that he expected that I came only to hurt him more. "Go away; I hate you and all your stupid talk!"

I continued to sit in silence for a while before softly saying, "Galen, you must really be hurting. I can't go away." His rejections continued, but with less volume and more sadness than anger. I wanted my silence to tell him he could give me all his rejection and hurt, if this was the only comfort he would allow.

A few more minutes passed before I asked Galen if he would let me come into his room. There was no answer. We shared a silence together; then I could hear his footsteps as he went to the door and unlocked it, and then quickly retreated to his bed. After a pause for peace to return, I thanked Galen for letting me into his room, and I opened the door. As soon as I entered, he gave me only a glimpse of his hurt, tearful, and frightened face, before frantically hiding under his covers. I closed the door, sat down with my back to the door, as far away from Galen as I could be, and thanked him again for letting me come in.

"I don't want to talk to you! You won't understand. Why don't you leave me alone?" Galen said in an agonized sob from under the covers. The rejections he was using so vigorously to protect himself were softening. After a long pause, I told him we didn't have to talk; I just wanted to hold him. Minutes passed before he made room in his bed for me and lifted the covers. I went to him and held him as he convulsed in tears. I told him how much I loved him and rode out the emotional storm with him.

How powerful and healing it is to simply hold and be present with someone in pain! We are all familiar with this yearning. Surely our Maker put it there, so that in our greatest darkness, we would not be alone. Galen soaked in the comfort of our embrace as a thirsty desert wanderer would take in cool well water. It revived him and restored peace and hope. Galen and I then talked about what had happened with his mother. He described how they had been opposing and rejecting each other. I felt sorrow for both of them, but especially for Galen who was hurt by his mother and hurt because he had hurt her. We talked together about how to make it better, obtain forgiveness, and prevent it from happening again. I talked with Gretchen and empathized with her hurt, and Galen's. I asked her if she could ask Galen to forgive her for what she had said to him that hurt;

and Galen sought her forgiveness. They made peace, and never again was there an incident like it.

> You belong to your father, the Devil, and you want to carry out your father's desire. He was a murderer from the beginning, not holding to the truth, for there is no truth in him. When he lies, he speaks his native language, for he is a liar and the father of lies. John 8:44

Rejection has permeated our being as yeast spreads throughout dough. It is the ultimate sin. It is the essence of sin itself. The archangel Lucifer first practiced it when he turned away from God, who created him and loved him, so he could "love" only himself. Fallen from heaven, Lucifer and a third of the angels took over the earth. As spiritual beings, we cannot see or hear them, just as we cannot see atoms or molecules; however, their influence in each of our lives and relationships is as real and far-reaching as the fundamental laws of physics. These demons know they are no match for God; however, the children of God are no match for them. What better way to hurt God than to hurt His children? And what better way to hurt is there than to destroy the loving connections between and among God and His children?

Look at rejection closely, and what do you see? You have a person who is alone, who is only concerned with obtaining what he desires. Other people only have value if they can be used to fulfill his desires. An act of deception is required to get around the free will or freedom of choice that people have. The practitioner of rejection must create the illusion that he is a legitimate judge of other people's value, worth, importance, capability, or lovability. He has to be believable. To succeed, he needs his victim to believe his judgments. In a way, he acts like he is God, the Supreme Being, the all-knowing, the holder of truth, the righteous judge. Of course, what is obviously missing is love.

With the power of illusion, pressure and force are put on other people to surrender what is desired. On one side is the attractive force of winning acceptance, and on the other is the painful punishment of rejection. People are fooled into believing they are good or bad, depending on their choice to give what is desired. This deception is truly artful, because the interaction involving giving and granting of acceptance has the look of loving. What is hidden is the deceiver's shallow motive of giving more importance to the desire than the person. The rejection can also be delivered artfully so that it appears merited to any observer, including the victim. More often than not, the rejection is delivered crudely, or even brutally, yet still with the air that it is deserved.

In the course of a day, each of us has hundreds of moment-to-moment desires of various kinds. It is our nature to give them more importance than we give to others' desires. Instantly and automatically, our minds busily search for ways to fulfill these desires and deliver them into conscious awareness. Going with the flow, we all are more likely to practice this grand illusion than to deliberately love and accept unconditionally with all the responsibilities implied. We are all born into pure egocentrism. The process of socialization is a practice of empathy, where time and time again we do what is counter to our nature, wait on our own desires, and care about the desires of others. Unfortunately, the agents of our socialization, more often than not, practice rejection themselves. Our nature, the world, and the powerful spiritual force of Satan conspire to create a reality of rejection, weakening our relationships with God, others, and ourselves. Both the giver and receiver of rejection suffer. The giver is sinking in a quicksand of self-comfort, cutting herself off more and more from loving. Some receivers withdraw and isolate for the sake of safety, unwittingly containing the poison that allows disease, confusion, helplessness, and hopelessness to flourish. Other receivers retaliate, attack, and take revenge with the same weapon that hurt them, thus becoming givers of rejection themselves.

It is not enough to accept others unconditionally; if we are to love, we must stand against rejection with all our might, joining forces with everyone we can, and most importantly with God.

> To those who sold doves he said, "Get these out of here! How dare you turn my Father's house into a market!" John 2:16

When Jesus went to the temple at Passover, He found the courts ripe with rejection. The temple in Jerusalem was the house of God, where His people could come to visit and worship. For many, it was a long and costly journey and could only be made once in a lifetime. For most, it was a high spiritual experience that deepened their faith. It was customary to bring sacrifices of animals they held dear for atonement and for the love of God. Upon reaching the temple, the faithful would find a market of men ready to exploit them. The priests' blessings could be obtained by bribes, and these men would sell "certifiably pure" sacrifices at exorbitant prices, after inspecting and rejecting the sacrifices the faithful brought with them. This coldly self-serving practice made a mockery of God and the people who loved Him. With passion, Jesus confronted rejection. He did not hurt or harm the men themselves; in fact, in a dramatic way He was extending a helping hand. In no uncertain terms, He showed them what they were doing was an abomination to God, His faithful people, and to themselves. The point of Jesus' attack was laser like on the act of rejection, the most formidable barrier to loving there is.

> Everyone who does evil hates the light, and will not come into the light for fear his deeds will be exposed. John 3:20

Rejection is the essence of evil. It is a choice, a method for obtaining what a person wants. It is conceived in the solitude and darkness of a person who is only thinking about himself. He prefers to keep what he is doing secret, so that he can more easily deceive his prey. He may fear what he is doing will come out into the open, ruining his chances for getting what he wants and activating condemnation.

Rejecting rejection is a loving act. It is a potent shield to set aside the rejection as a meaningless and valueless communication. To accept unconditionally and respect the giver of rejection is to offer him safety to reflect upon what he is doing and his choices. A loving person will lead the way peacefully in conversation about what is important to each person and how they may take care of that together. If the giver of rejection will not turn away from his hurtful method of getting what he wants, a loving person may leave standing an offer of forgiveness and the promise of a willingness to join with him, once he is able to set aside this evil way of treating people. This is, in fact, the way God relates with us as sinners. He does not reject us when we turn away from Him and pursue our selfish desires. Nor does He help us; rather, He allows us to face the consequences of our actions, including the loss of peace within and between others and ourselves. God is ready to forgive when we can turn away from our selfishness, and He welcomes us when we are willing to try the only other alternative to obtain what we want, loving.

> The world cannot hate you, but it hates me because
> I testify that what it does is evil. John 7:7

Hatred is a particularly hot and venomous form of rejection. It is a weapon to hurt the person who has withheld what another desires or who has become an obstacle as a result of pursuing her own desires, or even rights. On a surface level, the practitioner of hatred easily justifies her emotions and actions by blaming the victim. On a deeper level, hatred, like all rejection, is irrational. It requires a crazy, self-serving, and twisted leap of logic. To the person who hates, there is no justifiable reason for others to deny her what she wants. Her act of denial surrenders any value or worth she has as a human being, and it warrants painful punishment without any regard to "due process." The desire of the one who hates is given great importance, while the person in the way has no value. A single act that is despised transforms the actor—body, mind, and spirit—into a demon worthy of hatred and harm.

If we can appreciate this irrationality as a form of deception and see that hatred is a process of self-worship, along with the conditional acceptance and rejection of others, then we must admit that the prime force that drives hatred is none other than Satan, he who has rejected God and loving. The only value we have to Satan is as pawns in his campaign of hatred against God. He can use the willing, who are drawn to serve their desires, to wreak havoc with hatred, all the while concealing from them how he uses them for his own evil ambitions. As usual, Jesus tells us the truth. What is behind the hatred of people we know is Satan's hatred for Jesus. Jesus revealed the way Satan does business in relationships, condemned it, and showed us the great alternative of loving, which ultimately will put Satan out of business.

To be loving, we must follow Jesus' lead and condemn or reject acts of rejection in all their myriad forms. First and foremost, we must eliminate all the ways we have been rejecting God. With

Him, we have our most important relationship; however, no other relationship is more often denied or neglected. Sadly, most of the people who have ever lived have not developed a relationship with Him. Some have not believed He existed or have not wanted to have a relationship with Him. Others have decided to give their belief to one of the many false gods, such as money, power, fame, sex, drugs, rock and roll, pleasure, beauty, and so forth, ad nauseam. For many who do believe in Him, God is often relegated to the role of a minor character on the stage of their lives, thought of only for a few minutes on Sundays, Christmas, Easter, or when calamity visits. If only they knew Jesus was watching and listening to them all the time, waiting patiently, hoping He would be discovered as the ever-present companion, adviser, helper, healer, and lover they have always dreamed of having. How the fog of rejection can obscure the truth! Jesus has a passion for loving each one of us. It is a pure, perfect, powerful, and all-consuming passion. On His end, He makes sure nothing is in the way. If we will systematically reject everything except loving Him and others, He will give us the greatest of all loves, and we shall have the greatest joy of loving.

We need to purge ourselves of the ways we reject ourselves and devalue our heritage as children of God. Rejecting beliefs and thoughts about ourselves stick in our minds and disturb like splinters burrowed in our skin. Like splinters, they are foreign objects that truly do not belong to us. Our minds immediately generate disturbing emotions in hopes of calling our attention to the destructive and deceptive idea that we have accepted as true. Digging it out can be painful. Often we are tempted to just let it be. But, if we don't do anything about it, it will fester and poison us more and more as time goes on. Once we remove it, comfort is restored and healing can proceed. The forgiving love of Jesus is the ultimate medicine for healing. He offers us His truth in exchange for all the hurtful things we have come to believe and tell ourselves, such as, "No one loves me," "I'm no good," "I'm ugly," "I can't do anything right," "I'm stupid," "Other people are better than me," and others (you may consider your own personal rejections here). The truth is, each of us is a unique child of God. We exist because God desires an eternal loving relationship with us. We are so important to Him that He was willing to offer His own beloved Son, Jesus, as a sacrifice in death to save us. There is nothing that we could ever do to establish our worth and importance that could exceed these simple truths. He invites us to plant these seeds of truth in our minds, where they shall grow and flourish in loving with Him and others.

It is up to each of us to reject the ways we reject others. No one is going to do it for us. There is no excuse for treating people in ways we do not want to be treated. We are not God; we are in no position to judge the value and worth of other people. It is flat-out wrong to use other people to get what we want. Not only do we bring them harm, but we also immediately hurt ourselves whenever we are rejecting. On the surface, we often have the illusion that we are not being hurt, especially when we obtain what we want. Out of sight and out of mind, rejection spreads its ruinous reach throughout relationships and time. We lose love and the trust of others; our freedom, hope, peace, and joy; eventually our health and life; and worst of all, our very souls. We must be deliberate and purposeful on a moment-to-moment basis, practicing the great alternative to rejection, unconditional acceptance.

In our dealings with others, we are wise to reject any rejections given to us. We are not at the mercy of others, even though we are unable to control what they think, say, and do. We decide how much importance we shall give to the way people treat us. Compared to loving, rejection is worthless and meaningless. If we will only give importance to loving, we will not be hurt by rejection, and we will help those who are rejecting—first by showing them that their tactic to get what they want isn't working, and second, by modeling for them the superior alternative of loving. Rejecting the rejections of others is a process of compassion, forgiveness, and acceptance for the person and what is important to him, while setting aside the method he uses to obtain what he wants and offering the loving alternative.

When we reject God by pursuing our selfish desires, He surely is not offended. He understands we have no idea what we are doing, and in His love, He is concerned for us and will pursue us to return to Him. He readily will forgive us, if we seek it. He does not give importance to rejection, but to love. We should do the same when others reject us.

CHAPTER SEVEN

Hidden Treasure

As the Father has loved me, so have I loved you.
—John 15:9

Harvest time in the Maine wild blueberry fields is an epic canvas of the human soul. In the background is the beauty of summertime along the Maine coast. Pastel sunrises give way to a soft morning light that glistens in the morning dew. A dizzying array of insects and birds scrambles about the serious business of living, composing a symphony of celebration and tragedy. As the morning sun rises, the colors of the sky, forests, and fields play with one another to the delight of the eye. The air itself tastes pure and clean. Cool breezes stir the blood for working, but they will soon be spent as the sun heats the fields and humid air from the south sweeps up the coast. The middle of the day can be oppressive. Unprotected skin burns. Warm water bottles try to abate the thirst of bodies swimming in sweat. The backbreaking work of raking (sweeping the blueberry vines with eighteen-to-twenty-four-inch steel or aluminum combs with an open box on the back to collect the berries) slows as our energy is spent and we reach walls of fatigue, where the body refuses to move anymore and demands rest. Thankfully, on most days, the heat passes into a sepia soft light with cooler temperatures, reviving the rakers and boosting social interest. By the end of the day, everything is spent. Cool breezes return. The fields, the sky, and the rakers rest until the dawn.

The people working on this canvas come in all colors, shapes, and sizes. Although most are young, there are people of all ages. Some families with young children may leave older children to care for the younger ones, while their parents work in the fields. Twelve-to-sixteen-year-old students, who are not old enough to have a steady summer job, can make good money to spend as they fancy or to help with upcoming school expenses. The adults often are poor people with limited education and opportunity, living day-to-day, and season-to-season, doing work that no one else wants to do. They wear the hurt of their lives on their faces. There are a few who find it a refreshing break from routines of more or less satisfying vocations. Some are among the living dead, who know the torment of addiction, mental illness, violence, and imprisonment. More and more migrant workers from Mexico and Central America have been coming to work the larger farms or for a roving "crew boss" who contracts with small growers to clean their fields. Each of the rakers has a story and is in the midst of a stage and a moment of her life. For many, the past is a heavy weight, and the future is dark with scattered hope. There are the resilient, the carefree, the spirited, the playfully mischievous, the naïve, the ruthless, the lonely, the frightened, the high and self-promoted mighty, the victims and abusers, and the givers and takers, all mixed together for a month in the fields, and then gone. It is a month of labor, foolishness, drama, carnival, ugliness, hardship, conflict, opera, heroism, perseverance, kindness, cruelty, and beauty, washing through the coast of Maine like a tidal wave.

At the heart of it all are the sweet, dark blueberries, miraculous fruit that grows wild under harsh conditions and is brimming with healthy compounds. It is a fruit willing to give up its secrets to the curious about the gift of life, the elegant design of our Creator, the ordeal of survival, and the light that glows in each of us for loving.

BACK ON the path to the crossroads, the excitement of sharing the joy, peace, and love of the light with others is overflowing as the blessed make their way back. Some wonder why anyone hasn't come for them. Perhaps the revelation is new and they are among the first. Whatever the answer, it doesn't seem worth pursuing this question now. They have a wonderful mission. Each is making his way to the crossroads of his despair. Curious and peculiar things happen when they arrive. They see individual men and women alone, walking despondently in circles at the crossroads or lying in a heap on the ground. As they approach, it seems the people cannot hear their calls of greetings. At the end of the path, as they run jubilantly toward individual men and women, it seems they cannot be seen, even when the individual's gaze is in their direction. Most astounding of all, when they touch the person, their hands pass through their bodies as if through thin air. The individuals have no recognition of being touched or apparent awareness that anyone is there!

OH, HOW the Lord works in wondrous and loving ways, bringing others into our lives for mutual enrichment and giving us cause to behold His presence and glory! In 1987, when I was setting up a private psychology practice in a simple Cape Cod style house on the Penobscot River in Bucksport, Maine, I interviewed several women for a secretarial/bookkeeper position. One mature woman, who was not the most professional or the best typist of those I saw, stood out as the one to hire for reasons I could not explain well at the time. Her name was Nancy Maddocks; she was a faithful Christian woman, married to a good, hard-working man with whom she had raised two children, along with two nephews in need of a family and home. She was born and raised in Millinocket, Maine, a paper mill town and the gateway to the fabled Maine wilderness. Nancy was modest, direct, honest, hard-working, caring, and willing to learn. She was looking for more than a job. She wanted to do something that would touch peoples' lives.

She became the voice people would hear when they called for my help. She was the face and person they met when first visiting my office. She made people feel welcome and comfortable. She was my gatekeeper, protector of my time and the privacy so important for the people who came for help. She was also a voice for the people of Maine, teaching this Philadelphia flatlander about the heart and character of the people he was trying to help. She became a dear and important friend. Together, we went through many trials. Her mother developed a dementia that brought on a family crisis over how to care for her, as well as a bewildering passage through the rural system of care that was not prepared to help. She and her husband John were steadfast supporters of my family during our descent into the darkness of Gretchen's mental illness and death.

Nancy and John were a comfort to me as the traumas of Gretchen's life accumulated and gradually consumed her until she wasn't able to function occupationally. On most days, she was depressed and withdrawn, wishing she would die. It was hard for her to be a mother and a wife, which was all the more discouraging for her. In 1994, we reached a point where she could not dependably care for our twin sons, Galen and Christian, when they finished their day at school. I asked Nancy if she knew anyone who might provide afterschool childcare. She mentioned she had a niece who had recently returned to Maine from Texas, following a divorce, who might be interested in the job. On a hot summer afternoon, I met and interviewed Nancy's niece at our home. Her name was Theresa. She parked an old, rusty, maroon Chrysler in front of our garage and introduced herself with a warm smile and a slight Texas accent. She was living with her parents and her three children, having recently returned to Maine, where she had grown up. She was dedicating her time to being a mother but was looking for a way to make some money without compromising the attention she wanted to give her children following her divorce and move. She was very understanding and compassionate as I spoke to her about my wife and our children's needs. She would pick my children up at school and care for them in her home until I was able to pick them up after work. It was an ideal match for both of us. My sons would be cared for in a family setting by a caring mother, and Theresa would have a part-time job doing what she loved to do in her own home. Over the next three years, my sons developed a beautiful attachment to Theresa and her parents and gradually were becoming members of their family. Every day after work during the school year, I would drop by her home, pick up my sons, and exchange pleasantries. The boys would have their homework done and often would have eaten supper with the Hileman family. My sons and I were able to go home and spend some quality time together, and with Gretchen. This routine went on until the fall of 1997. For the most part, what I knew about Theresa and her family, I learned from my sons. With the exception of occasional squabbles with her children, the boys were content and thriving in her care.

At the same time Gretchen was diagnosed with cancer, Theresa's mother and Nancy's sister, Barbara, also was diagnosed with cancer. Gretchen and Barbara had the same doctor and radiation treatments together. Theresa, Barbara, and Gretchen were bound with one another in a fight for their lives. The extraordinary caring Theresa had given our sons had deeply touched Gretchen. Theresa had won Gretchen's trust and respect and then had become one of the few people in the world who simply loved her. Theresa gave all of herself to Gretchen, just as she gave all of herself to her mother. Theresa, of course, shared her greatest treasure with Gretchen, her love for Jesus. In one of the most remarkable moments of their lives, while deeply in prayer together, Gretchen stepped into the presence of Jesus, and the radiant light of His love and glory healed her heart and soul. Afterward, like giddy little girls, Gretchen and Theresa danced for joy. Gone was all the hurt of Gretchen's life. Her sadness and fear were gone. Her wish to die was replaced by a passion to live only for love. From that moment on, Gretchen was with Jesus. Theresa and Gretchen, in a sudden and dramatic way, had transcended friendship and become sisters.

Theresa and her family were a steady and comforting presence for our family in the days that followed. The children continued the reassuring and loving routine they had known for years in the Hileman home. I was able to love and care for my wife at home for much of her illness, because behind the scenes, quietly, Theresa was there. I was the only member of our family who did not truly know her. She remained in the background while Gretchen passed away and I went into grief.

ONE OF the most profound questions all of us struggle with throughout our lives is about our value and worth. If it is not present in our awareness, then it will ramble on in the background of our minds, as if searching for definitive truth. Many confuse this question with how other people treat them or how capably they manage the affairs of their lives. The standards by which people measure worth can be like shifting sands; moment-to-moment and situation-to-situation, our evaluations and those of others mysteriously change as if there is no truth. Some people may hold a set of standards for decades, or even a lifetime, certain they are true, only to find out in crisis or at the hour of their death that their standards were a mirage. It is easy to become preoccupied with ourselves, living in our skins and our heads as we do. It's not easy to get away from ourselves. Everywhere we go, there we are. We are absorbed in our experiences and our river of desires. We receive immediate feedback for everything we do. Sometimes our intentions and plans work out, but it is probably fair to say that results fall short of our expectations most of the time, and we must try again or clean up a mess. It is peculiar that many people do not seem to know that all of this has nothing to do with their value and worth. In fact, it is rather amazing our plans work out as often as they do. After all, there is much more going on than meets the eye when we learn something new or develop further skills for interacting in the world; besides, the world is also far more complicated than it looks.

Take something as simple as communicating a message to someone. To accurately transfer from one mind to another what is meant or felt in the heart is no small undertaking. By virtue of our unique life experience, each of us has nuances of meaning associated with nearly every word and gesture. What are the chances that if I say the word *blue* to you, we will have exactly the same shade of blue in mind? Ask other people, what does love mean? You will very likely hear a unique definition from everyone you ask. While many people may find it a nuisance and miserable to have to work so hard to get things done or to communicate with other people, it is actually a blessing in disguise.

It is a natural and universal condition that our limitations are omnipresent and endless. The list of what each of us does not know and cannot do goes on infinitely. Happily, we are all in the same boat when it comes to limitations. Certainly, the nature of our limitations varies from unique person to unique person. Our collective insecurities about what we don't know or can't do promote a snobbishness of knowledge, as if it is valid and legitimate to compare our experiences with one another's. As if "objectively" one person's experience really is more important and valuable than others'. In an effort to ease doubts about their worth and value, many people unconsciously sell their knowledge and themselves as being superior to others. There also are many who have come to believe that they and their experience are less important.

The blessings of limitations are humility and respect. In humility, we receive a grand comfort, peace, security, and confidence. Our limitations guarantee that no one is better or less than anyone else. Since they are endless for everyone, limitations are no big deal, and they certainly are not grounds for evaluating our worth and value. On the contrary, when we face one of our limits, we have an opportunity for loving, the only activity that can reveal the truth about our priceless worth and value. When we do not know something or cannot do something, we have a choice. We can labor alone creatively, experimentally, or experientially to try to find or discover the information or ability we desire, or we can join together with others who may already have the information we seek and explore possibilities together in complementary and collaborative teamwork. The former may help an individual develop talents and may be useful as a prelude to collaborative teamwork. It can be tempting, however, to use this solitary labor to cultivate pride, which ultimately isolates people and draws them away from the truth. Young children are naturals at seeking help when they are at their limits. Helping them is a mutually loving experience that everyone can enjoy. Conditional acceptance and rejection gradually erode children's spontaneous exuberance for learning, making their learning a serious test of their value and worth, thus instilling anxiety over their limitations. Joining with others to go beyond a limit can transform a mundane need for information or a momentary need for achievement into a binding, endearing, loving celebration of mutual respect.

> How can you believe, if you accept praise from
> one another, yet made no effort to obtain the
> praise that comes from the only God? John 5:44

Jesus cautions us about giving importance to the praise of others. While we may like it, feel good about ourselves, and feel closer to the people who offer it to us, it can be deceiving. It could fool us into thinking our worth and value depend upon what we know, what we can do, or our ability to please others. It can deceive us into thinking other people are legitimate judges of our worth and value. If we fall for this, we will be taking a journey down the Way of Happiness after the signs have been switched. Instead, Jesus directs us to seek the praise of God, our loving Creator and Father, who established our true worth and value by giving us life as one of His children. It is vitally important that we all understand this. We are alive because God Himself loves us and wants us to be with Him, forever in loving. It is astounding beyond our wildest dreams that the Almighty Creator of the universe values us, all of us, so deeply. And He feels this way, despite our infinite limitations. In this light, it truly doesn't matter how other people, with all their limitations, judge our value and worth, because the basis for our entitlement to respect was established irrevocably by God. Therefore, He is the only one worthy of our praise and profound thankfulness, and He is the only One whom we must please, whose praise really matters. There is no doubt; the greatest treasure we all possess is God's love. It is the tragedy of the human race that almost all of us have no idea we have it.

> A new command I give to you: Love one another.
> As I have loved you, so you must love one another.
> John 13:34

What could more securely establish our worth than to be objects of God's love? We receive this treasure at the moment of our creation, our conception. We shall always have it, unless we deliberately give it up. Who in their right mind would tell God His love is unwanted? Would such a person truly understand what she was doing? In the midst of the hurt and disappointments in loving with other people, it is understandable that we would reject "love." In fact, we would find it hard to conceive how God could love us, because we would not have a frame of reference in our day-to-day lives. Jesus gives us our only frame of reference in His own life. Through two thousand years of babbling human cultures, His life and teachings have been preserved faithfully in the Bible. His voice is clear and strong, cutting to the heart of all matters. Here He gives us a command for the sake of emphasis. He wants us to be focused. He wants to make it simple. We are all objects worthy of His love and the love of each other. If we will follow His command and actively love others, we will live well and fully. In His love, we are all equals; no one is more or less important than anyone else. The good fortune, achievements, status, power, fame, and personal glory we may accrue in this life do not matter in the grand scheme of eternity. God's love and loving are all that matter. It is God who has made us lovable. We are so valuable to God that He would send His only Son to save us and die in our place so that we could be with Him forever. Surely, all of us deserve respect from everyone else and, more importantly, have a responsibility to respect everyone else. When we treat each other as priceless equals, we get a glimpse of the profound and perfect love between the Father and Jesus, as well as the love they have for us.

To be unconditionally and humbly accepting and respectful of others as fellow siblings of God establishes vibrant, safe, secure, and trustworthy connections between people. This is the basis for dependability, loyalty, and faithfulness in relationships. It gives relationships hope.

In this verse Jesus asks us to contemplate how He has loved us in every word and deed. In the three short years of His public ministry, He taught us how to love by way of His parables and teachings. He showed by example how to live in a loving relationship with His Father. With a sweeping array of people of all ages, backgrounds, educations, statuses, and stations of living, facing all manner of human predicaments, Jesus answered the question once and for all: how do you love? Permeating His loving like the fragrance of perfume was His humble respect. He completely, purely, and simply valued His Father and His people. In our selfishness and concern for fulfilling our desires, we are arrogant, impatient, and foolishly unaware of how we are discarding hidden treasure for a worthless momentary comfort. If we cannot humbly respect another, it is unlikely we will be trusted; thus, we set up encounters of conflict, where force rather than loving will prevail.

> In my Father's house are many rooms; if it were not so, I would have told you. I am going there to prepare a place for you. And if I go and prepare a place for you, I will come back and take you to be with me that you also may be where I am. You know the way to the place where I am going.
> John 14:2–4

As Jesus spoke these words, not one of the apostles could imagine or comprehend what He was telling them. To prepare a place for them and us, He would go through the passion, conquering sin, Satan, and death to be with His Father and open the rooms of His Father's house to us. Then He would come back for us, so that we could be with Him and know that the way to the place where He had gone was by following Him. He valued His Father and us infinitely—so much so that the Almighty living God humbled Himself to become one of us and take on the collective hatred and rejection of all humankind. He went through unspeakable agony. He endured the complete reversal of His nature, becoming sin. Worst of all was the excruciating separation from His loving Father. His ultimate and final sacrifice on our behalf was the only way for love to flourish between the Father and His children. Jesus came to us and for us, so that we could be with Him and with our Father. Jesus was and is profoundly "there for us." Even though He lived two thousand years ago, it is as true today as it was then. What He did gives great depth to the act of respect. He showed us how to respect our Father, and others. For the sake of glorifying His Father and blessing our lives, He gave us the command to practice respect His way, the way to be with Him.

The practice of respect and valuing others by the way we treat them will immediately bless us with the presence and the protection of Jesus, with His peace, love, and joy. Don't take my word for it. Simply watch how you feel when you unselfishly and humbly treat another person as a priceless child of God. Joy of joys! Know also that this is how you deserve to be treated by everyone. In fact, whenever you are not treated this way, you can take comfort that Jesus respects you perfectly, and you will know instantly that the other person has become lost in himself and very much needs someone to show him the way. By giving him the respect he deserves and asking for it in return, we show him another way of being with people, Jesus' way. He will, of course, have the choice to join you in mutual respect or to continue on his way alone with all its misery. By requiring the respect of others and ourselves, we will be safe, and we will show others the presence of Jesus in us, our hidden treasure.

CHAPTER EIGHT

Peace

In this world, you will have trouble. But take
heart! I have overcome the world.

—John 16:33

A T THE crossroads, there are now two. One is a woman, hopelessly
defeated and discouraged, and you who have returned for her,
overflowing with joy and hope. A mysterious barrier lies between
you, rendering the woman alone and rendering you invisible and
unable to help. As you watch her, memories and the emotions
of being alone at the crossroads come flooding back. An aching
compassion moves you to find a way of freeing her from misery.
At first, gently and softly, you try whispering and touching her
forlorn face. You offer words of comfort, affection, friendship,

of good news, and an invitation to come away with you to the light, while reverently holding the face of the dispirited woman in your hands. There is no reaction, not a blink of the eye, not even the slightest movement of face or body. She does not hear you or feel your touch. She is stuck, frozen in place, almost statuesque, except for a wave of the hand to shoo away a fly. You will have to try harder and find another way.

You go down the Path of Doom and gather up all the beautiful flowers and delicious fruits you can carry. You lay them at the feet of the woman, sitting in hopelessness. They are simply beautiful, luminescent in color and fragrance. The fruit is so appealing you can't resist peeling a sweet juicy orange and taking a wedge of it to your mouth, while offering her a slice. *Surely*, you think, *these dazzling treats for the senses will awaken and refresh this woman who seems asleep in misery.* Slowly, she rises to her feet, pushing the ground with her hands to stand, and then walks over and through the flowers and fruit. She scratches her back as she walks away in oblivion, without disturbing anything underfoot, and you can hardly believe your eyes. *What will it take to reach her?*

When the sun begins to set, you will make your next move. She's walking around the crossroads, lingering at the head of each path, kicking the dirt, mumbling under her breath, and occasionally looking down the paths in a daze. You decide you will take her forcefully. You will wait until she next approaches the Path of Doom, and then you will pick her up and carry her down the path until she can see the beautiful light glowing brilliantly in the darkness. She leans against the post of the Way of Happiness sign, looking down the path and fidgeting with her hands. Suddenly, she runs quickly down the path. Aghast, you run after her, hoping to save her, but not knowing how. As you run, fear fills your throat, beats your heart, and pumps your legs. At any moment you expect violence and terror to appear. Out of the darkness come others who are running after the woman. She glances back and runs harder, but you can see she is tiring and will not be able to stay ahead for long. You are able to run alongside and even pass some of those who chase her. They run with strength and menace, hundreds of them pouring out of the darkness and onto the path, each one fiercely obsessed with catching her. None seem to notice you are there running among them.

She is just ahead now. The demons are about to take her. She is screaming for her life. One last time, she looks over her shoulder and then stumbles and falls. In just a moment, a swarm of them piles on top of her, squealing with excitement. You take three more steps and dive into the pile. As you leave the ground, in your heart you speak to the light: "I am alone, afraid, and don't know what will happen now. Please save us!"

At that moment in the air, you are filled with the brilliantly radiating light. You slice like a white-hot sword through the squirming frenzied pile of demons and sweep up the woman in your arms as the light drains all strength from the swarm. Together in the light, you are lifted above the path, and a soft, gentle wind carries you together back to the crossroads, where you are left in peace.

WHEN GRETCHEN and I bought the blueberry land in 1987, our twin sons, Christian and Galen, were only one year old. We had been living in a simple three-room house that was nestled in the woods. The location appealed to Gretchen for its privacy and sense of safety. But for Gretchen, this was one more dream that would become a nightmare. We had been married for eight years and very much wanted to have a child. Gretchen had been plagued by recurring fibroid tumors in her uterus, which compromised the attachment of fertilized ova to the uterine wall. She felt time was running out on her dream of having a child. For years she had harbored tender fantasies of having a daughter. She would call her Emily. She had taken to collecting antique dolls and even dressing up our West Highland terrier dogs and Persian cat in infants' clothing. Her heart longed for a child. Month after month, we rode a roller coaster of emotion, scurrying to conceive when the calendar and her temperature told us it was the moment, only to dissolve in bitter sadness at the coming of her period. Her menstrual cycles were erratic, intensely painful, and emotionally dark. The disappointment of being unable to conceive had the power to raise up thoughts of suicide. I admit many times feeling hopeless and helpless as I tried to comfort Gretchen.

Cast into this pot were dashes of trauma and terror. Our neighbor's teenage sons, who enjoyed hunting, knew Gretchen's passion for nature and the sacredness of wildlife. One day, they sent her a message. As Gretchen went out to the woodshed one morning, she found the decapitated torsos of two mallard ducks. Emotionally, it was like discovering murdered children. Gretchen strongly identified the vulnerability of animals with the abuses of humankind. She was enraged and profoundly saddened. A piece of her died with the mallards. This event shattered her sense of safety in our home. She felt that without warning other terrors would strike. And, she was right.

Always very gradually, Gretchen would regain her emotional balance. Together, we were determined to conceive a child. We sought out fertility treatments. For months, we pushed ourselves through lovemaking that was more like work than pleasure. At last, the miracle we had hoped for happened. Gretchen was pregnant!

Our hearts overflowed with joy for a season. Like a couple of birds, we began preparing a nest. As the pregnancy unfolded, however, anxieties also grew. Would Gretchen be able to carry the child to term with the fibroids? Would her dream of having a daughter be fulfilled? Privately, I worried and hoped. Could the pregnancy be uneventful medically, emotionally, and spiritually? Could we find an oasis of peace?

On a cold January morning, after letting our West Highland terriers, Muffie and Beau, out for a run and some fun, they curiously did not respond to our calls to come home. Muffie was a sweet, affectionate, and loyal dog who softened Gretchen's grief after Brit was killed. Beau was a real boy—stocky, playful, and always game. We both went out searching the woods around our home, checking the many trails and their favorite haunts. They were nowhere to be seen. In desperation, Gretchen called our friend, Larry Baum, a Coast Guard lighthouse keeper with a pilot's license. Larry took Gretchen up in his plane to look for the dogs. On the first pass over our house, there they were, floating lifelessly on the neighbor's ice rimmed pond. They had gone out on the ice after mallards, fallen through, and hadn't been able to get out. Gretchen was instantly catapulted into a state of torment. It was as if she had seen her own children drown from the sky. Her grief was so overwhelming that she was sickened for weeks. All I could do was hold her, ride out the monstrous storm of emotion, and again share my own grief with her. A light snow fell that day. The wind blew an eerie sound through the trees as I dug a shallow grave for our beloved dogs, burying them with my tears and a fervent prayer for God to take care of Gretchen and me.

The recovery from this heartbreak in the dead of winter, three months into the pregnancy, was painfully slow. Increasingly Gretchen looked to the future with foreboding. Her youth was gone. All the important relationships of her life, except ours, gave her more pain than joy. At times, the weight of expectations on our relationship was too much to bear, and I, too, hurt her. My yearning for a simple, peaceful love with Gretchen seemed always out of reach. My fear that this weight might be placed on our unborn child or that another demon of disappointment was coming were dark, heavy weights on my spirit.

After a couple of months, Gretchen went to look at some golden retriever puppies. In part, we thought it would be good for our child to grow up with a dog whose breed was known to be good with children; but also, unspoken, we were looking for healing and a ray of hope. The puppies worked their magic on us, and we left with a feisty female we named Dinah. About a week later, we received news that shifted the plates of our beings. Gretchen was carrying twins.

Naturally, we felt joy at the prospect of having two children after the ordeal of trying to conceive. As we tried to absorb the ramifications of this news for an already risky pregnancy, and for the doubling of responsibility when we were emotionally weary, questions and fears came flooding in. An ultrasound revealed the need for surgery to remove the fibroids from the uterus, as they were threatening the pregnancy. Of course, the surgery was not without risk. After passing this challenge, Gretchen went on to gain eighty pounds, developed preeclampsia, went through Braxton Hicks contractions, and endured relentless discomfort and sleep deprivation. A few weeks before her due date, she begged her doctor on her knees, "Cut these babies out of me!"

For the safety of the newborns and Gretchen, a C-section was performed, with four doctors and two nurses attending. Thankfully, all went well, with one exception. Both of the infants were boys. Gretchen's dream of having a daughter was lost. She found it difficult for the first few weeks to find love for them, and yet here they were, two completely helpless little people in need of our care around the clock. At one of the grandest moments of life, Gretchen was again a prisoner of grief. I surrounded her with family and friends, and I welcomed and sought help in all shapes and sizes for young Galen and Christian, as well as for Gretchen and myself.

In time, the boys captured Gretchen's heart, and plans began forming to buy some land and build a new home and future together. About a year later, we spent every penny we had to buy one hundred acres of blueberry fields and woods we called Highland. It was more than we could afford, but it was a dream we could not resist. One beautiful summer morning, Gretchen, Christian, Galen, and I, along with Dinah and a spunky Westie named Mimi, played and had a picnic together on a field at Highland, where we would build our home. It was our first taste of peace.

MAKING PEACE with ourselves, others, and God is another essential ingredient of loving. Peace is also one of the fruits of love, which nourishes continued loving and lays down seed for future love. Peace flows from acceptance and respect, yet it requires attention, care, and cultivation. We cannot expect or depend on others to bring it, or give it, except for one, Jesus. With His peace, we have perfect safety, security, and calm, no matter what our circumstances may be. At best, we can only manage a fleeting sense of peace on our own—a momentary peace that is bound to circumstances or the good graces of others. Jesus gives peace abundantly—a profound, deep, and enduring peace that can be shared with others. The peace of Jesus heals, protects, comforts, banishes all fear, invites forgiveness, and opens the gates for loving. His peace makes us peacemakers. With His peace, loving our enemies is possible.

My childhood of hurt grew into a youth of insecurity. To a large extent, I came to believe I was an unwanted and unloved child who was bad and stupid. I was determined to hide these awful feelings, because I was sure other people would find out and painfully reject me. This was a setup for a vicious cycle. As long as I protected myself by keeping others at a distance, I was alone with the awful beliefs and feelings, which were growing into my identity as I matured. Inside me, the classic conflict of good and evil raged. Every so often, I would act in bad and stupid ways, strengthening the grip of the hurtful beliefs. I could not free myself from this web and was afraid to let anyone help.

Amazingly, help came for me. At first, it was neighbors and friends; then it was a few teachers, a guidance counselor, a school principal, a few college professors, a priest, women who loved me when I didn't know how to love, fellow graduate students, and a few special mentors. I felt unworthy and lucky. I had no way of knowing it then, but looking back and seeing how each of these people were placed in my path at the right moment, when I could have easily been swallowed up by the hurt, I know this was the hand of God. He was calling me to the loving I so desperately needed.

Two important milestones along the way were forgiving my mother and father and seeking the forgiveness of my younger brother Paul, whom I had hurt. As a child, my relationship with my parents contained much sadness and fear. As an adolescent, it grew into anger and defiance. As a young man, I came to blame them for my unhappiness. However, as others showed me that they loved me, it became clear that I had no one to blame for my unhappiness but myself. My parents had hurt me out of their loving intentions and limitations. I realized I needed their forgiveness as much as they needed mine. I had hoped and, for a time, waited for my parents to begin the process of forgiveness. When it did not come, I had to dig deep for courage and go to them. They received me with love, and together we made peace.

More than anyone, I gave my own hurt as a child to my younger brother Paul. He was a handsome, sweet boy, who seemed to have our mother's favor. Perversely, it felt good to tease him and bully him, even though I knew it was wrong. When caught, I would face my mother's punishment. I was desperate for a way to feel important and powerful. Hurting Paul was the best I could do, until I made enough friendships to have a life away from my family. Like a thief, I had stolen his peace. As the love came to me from others, my regret and remorse for what I had done to Paul grew. He went out into the world and lived adventurously, traveling the world, challenging himself, looking for love and peace. On a beautiful summer morning, we walked on the beach of Longport, New Jersey, where we had summered together as children. I expressed my sorrow to him for what I had done as a child to hurt him and asked for his forgiveness. In an emotional embrace he gave me this precious gift, and together we shared peace.

The relationship between forgiveness and loving is profound. Forgiveness is a loving act. It heals, settles, resolves, and restores connection, safety, and trust. It creates peace and offers the opportunity for a new beginning. It opens the way for loving. Unfortunately, like loving itself, forgiveness can be perverted. When our hearts are not in it, saying we are sorry may be an empty, shallow, and selfish act, or it can be a tool of manipulation to obtain something we want from others. When we practice this kind of forgiveness, we can cause others to be suspicious, jaded, and unforgiving. We can confuse and make it difficult for others to tell whether our forgiveness is genuine or not. How foolish it is to weaken this great force for loving! Without the peace forgiveness can provide, we are doomed to live miserably alone. Without forgiveness, we have no redemption, no way of overcoming our mistakes, sins, and the hurt we have caused others, and no way of saving and loving people who have hurt us. Forgiveness dispels darkness with radiant light.

> For the bread of God is He who comes down from
> heaven and gives life to the world. John 6:33

Jesus came into the world as the only one capable of forgiveness in order to restore the peace that was lost when humankind turned away from God to indulge in selfish desires. By the sacrifice of His own life, He gave life to the world. There is only death in our selfishness. When we only care about our moment-to-moment desires, we cheapen the value of other people and of loving itself, while squandering our own worth. It is as if our desires matter more than anything. They become the gods we worship. There is no peace in this. On the contrary, living for our desires is at best a restless, disturbing, and elusive search for peace. The illusion is that peace is just around the corner, perhaps a moment away, within reach.

The life of Jesus and His teachings place the search for peace in its proper perspective. He is the source of true peace. Only when our relationship with Him becomes the most important and central relationship in our day-to-day lives will we have His peace. When we come to think of Him more often than anyone else in our lives; when we talk with Him and listen from our hearts about all the matters, great and small, concerning us; when we rest in and enjoy His faithful companionship; and when we love Him and others for His glory, we will have a secure and peaceful base from which to live in this world. We will be able to face anything without fear. We will never be alone. The rejections and judgments of others will be meaningless. His peace fills us with compassion and gives us the power to be forgiving.

> Do not let your hearts be troubled. Trust in God;
> trust also in me. John 14:1

Surely it is difficult to trust others and even to trust ourselves. How we yearn to find people we can trust and to be trusted ourselves! Trust helps us feel safe and secure, and it helps us have peace. Yet, we know even the people we trust the most in our lives have the potential to let us down, just as we can disappoint others in our moments of weakness and selfishness. We all have had countless experiences with others in which either they, we, or all of us cared more about our desires than we cared about each other. We have been conditioned. We have learned. We have come to believe that we are wise to be careful about trusting others. We all have had our moments when we trusted someone with complete vulnerability and were devastatingly hurt. At the time, the hurt was painful, shocking, and disturbing, perhaps taking days or weeks to recover from. But, as time goes on, the hurt is muted and grows into caution, which subtly isolates us from others and complicates our search for peace and love. In our isolation, we are drawn to care more about fulfilling our desires to find comfort than we are to find true peace and love. Thus, a vicious cycle grows.

Truly, the only one it can be completely safe for us to trust is our God who made us. He is the perfect Father, who loved us so much that He gave His Son to die for us, so we could be with Him forever in peace and love. Certainly, we are unaccustomed to trusting someone we cannot see, hear, or touch. In contrast to our daily experience in a sensual reality, trusting on the basis of faith can be a real stretch. There is no shortage of naysayers, who will ridicule belief and trust in God. After all, we are living in a fallen world. However, the history that we are provided in the Bible has been proven as accurate as any other source time and time again. Jesus is a historical figure. He proved He was who He said He was by fulfilling hundreds of predictions or prophecies perfectly, and to the moment. In fact, He fulfilled all the predictions that spanned thousands of years before His birth to the letter, no more and no less. This was no psychic, prophet, or spiritually enlightened man. This was God. Not only is it safe to trust and believe in Him and what He said and did, it is foolish not to. There will always be skeptics. The Bible itself recognizes that after the fall of Adam and Eve there have always been people who do not believe in God. Jesus in the flesh faced all the powers of His time, political and religious, who were so threatened by Him and His message and so incapable of believing Him that they very nicely conformed to the predicted script devised by God at the beginning of time, and they cruelly put Him to death. By comparison, today's skeptics, who have the impediment of two thousand years to forget, distort, and confuse, are amateurs. Indeed, compare those who believe and love Jesus with those who do not, and notice the difference there is in their peace. Jesus has shown us that He is more real and true than anything we will ever know. Trust Him, and you will receive true peace.

> Remain in me, and I will remain in you. No branch can bear fruit by itself; it must remain in the vine. Neither can you bear fruit, unless you remain in me. John 15:4

Keeping our cool with other people is a prerequisite for success. Our calm can be contagious. Our calm is a base of strength. Without calm, people will be on guard, connections will be weak or non-existent, and thus, it will be difficult, if not impossible to accomplish anything. Without calm, the chances of communicating accurately what we mean, feel, or want are nil. In the absence of calm, people will always pay more attention to how messages are sent than to the messages themselves. We invite people to resist and oppose us if we are not calm.

If something is important to us, if there is urgency, we are inclined to put pressure on others to pay attention, stop whatever they are doing, listen, and give us what we want. Whenever we act this way, however, peace goes out the window. Tension and pressure are also contagious, often in an escalating way. The biochemistry of tension involves the secretion of adrenaline and cortisol rapidly into the blood stream. These "stress hormones" can shut down the thinking part of the brain and divert the flow of blood into the muscles to ready the body for "fight or flight". Often this will lead to a breakdown of communication and teamwork between people. It will preclude any hope of understanding or resolution. With tension, the deck is stacked for frustration, defeat, or hurt.

Parents, teachers, counselors, friends, and self-help books tell us over and over how important it is to calm down. We are treated to a large assortment of advice, techniques, and strategies for calming down. No doubt, calming is a matter of temperament and skill, which could be practiced and developed. It is quite common, however, to see even the most practiced having a breaking point, where they simply can't keep their cool. They know what to do. They know how important it is. They have done it many times before, even in some very challenging situations. But, there are times, places, situations, and people where the mighty masters of calm will fall, because we are all human, robust with our infinite limitations.

There is something deep, mysterious, and profound in us that is vital for being calm. People who have been hurt deeply by others, who do not want to be hurt again, will show you. Overwhelming hurt can make calm impossible, at least with other people. The ever-present anxiety is like an alarm that will not go off, requiring vigilance for hurt that may happen unpredictably at any moment. The coping skills, techniques, and practice of calming are just Band-Aids. The most hurt among us clearly reveal a need we all have for a deeper, more powerful "medicine" to live calmly in peace.

> Again Jesus said, "Peace be with you! As the Father has sent me, I am sending you." And with that He breathed on them and said, "Receive the Holy Spirit." John 20:21–22

Calm and peace are not states of being that we can impose on others or ourselves. If our inner peace depends upon having peace around us, we will live with some measure of vulnerability and helplessness. Peace on the surface is neither strong nor endurable. If we think that other people or even ourselves are the critical actors for achieving and maintaining peace, we are mistaken. It takes two, helping each other. Each has a responsibility for peacemaking that involves a stewardship of oneself and an offering of guidance and help to the other. It is wise to let others know what they can do to facilitate peace. It is vital to find out and act on what would help others establish peace. Even the Prince of Peace, Jesus, cannot give us peace unless we are willing to receive it by faith in Him.

The deepest union possible for peace that we could have is with the Holy Spirit, God in spirit, living within everyone who believes and loves Jesus. Think about this. The Spirit of God desires to live within you, inseparably, to become one with you, creating a foundation of peace for your life. In the fertile soil of this peace, the Spirit offers moment-to-moment guidance for the love of God and others. This is the greatest deal for peace there could ever be. By comparison, our part is small, humble, and insignificant. We must exercise our free will to love Jesus and to be open to receive the Holy Spirit, who then does the "heavy lifting" of transforming us from the lost and loveless to become the loving equivalent of Jesus. The Spirit knows long before we do what we need. Indeed, He knows and understands us completely. He is perfectly aware, attuned, passionately interested, and caring. He is ever ready to guide us wherever we may be and humble to the point of invisibility so as to direct our full attention to Jesus. With the Spirit, the depths of our being are filled to overflowing with the peace of Jesus.

It probably is obvious that with the profound peace we can obtain together with the Holy Spirit, it becomes natural to exude and inspire calm and peace in others. The conflicts, disturbance, and rejections of others cannot weaken our peace; on the contrary, they empower it. As we become as loving as Jesus, we will forgivingly separate love from noise, appreciate the deeper needs of others, and humbly offer loving guidance by the way we treat others. Our peace extends an invitation to others to share in it and then join us in an experience of loving.

The peace Gretchen and I had in the blueberry field at Highland with our sons and pets on that beautiful summer day was fleeting. Sadness and pain would become frequent visitors in the years ahead. No matter how hard we tried, alone and together, peace was elusive. On September 17, 1997, not even two weeks after Gretchen received the terminal diagnosis, peace came for us. The moment Gretchen stood before Jesus, He gave her His peace, which she shared with me. Ever since, I have been blessed with His peace and love.

CHAPTER NINE

The Gift

He who belongs to God hears what God says. The reason you do not hear is that you do not belong to God.

—John 8:47

THE WOMAN and you lie in a deep sleep at the crossroads, where the light has left you together in peace. After a time, you wake together, she in a state of confusion and you in unfamiliar clarity. Her confusion is peculiar for the absence of fear. Her mind is buzzing with questions, but she feels a calm she has never known before, which seems so out of place. It is surprising and soothing at the same time. She is a woman not easily given to trust people, but now she feels utterly safe with you, someone she never met before, who literally came out of nowhere. "Who are you?" she asks with a touch of awe. "Where are we? What happened?" She looks at you intently, impatient to hear your response.

As you look into her eyes, you know that at last she can see you. In fact, you are experiencing a connection and openness with the woman that is hard to describe, beyond simply complete. You can hear her questions, but more remarkably, you can feel her emotions and understand her desires. You do not have to speak to her. The light in you answers in a voice that speaks to her heart and spirit.

"I am a friend, like you, who was once lost at the crossroads of life where we each make the only choice that matters. I came back for you, because I once hoped someone would come for me."

It is surreal for the woman to receive your reply in the depths of her being as she looks upon your face, which radiates kindness and gentleness. *How did he do that?* she wonders to herself, her curiosity taking over confusion.

"Why did you come back for me? I don't even know you."

The light in you answers, "Yes, we don't know each other in any way but one, which is more important than anything. I have the light you were looking for."

"I don't understand. What light?"

The voice of the light tells her to lie down and close her eyes. In her stillness and peace, the question arises from within: "Above all else, what do you really want?"

She understands that when an answer comes, she is to open her eyes. Her mind is racing. Her first thought is, *How should I know?* Then a stream of memories flows through her mind: a mix of wonderful moments of happiness, as well as moments of darkness. Her life is flashing before her eyes. You can see it all and feel it all. She has the peculiar sense that you are experiencing it with her. You know her answer a moment before she speaks and opens her eyes.

"Perfect love forever."

As her eyes open, they are filled with the light. Without saying a word, you take her hand, help her up, and together you walk down the path with the sign, The Path of Doom.

IN 1988 Theresa became a Christian. By September of 1993, Theresa's ten-year marriage was careening to an end. Six months earlier, she had given birth to their third child, a daughter named Whitney. Theresa pursued her husband in hopes of restoring their marriage. It wasn't to be. Suddenly, Theresa and her three children were left with little more than her faith. One day, when her family was without food, Theresa prayed to Jesus, asking for His help. Out of the blue a woman from her church visited with several large shopping bags of food, telling Theresa, the Lord had "put it on my heart" to bring the groceries. For five years, Theresa waited, hoped, and trusted in Jesus. He became her husband for a time. In her heart, she longed for Jesus to bring her a faithful and loving man. He was listening and preparing Theresa, as well as the man He would bring to her.

LISTENING TO the blueberry fields through the seasons of the year is an uncommon pleasure. Spring is a symphony of wind, songbirds, buzzing bees, and crickets on an expansive stage of rolling hills, forest, and blue sky, celebrating the renewal of life, the fulfillment of promises, and faithfulness. Standing in the field, taking it all in, the message resonates in my soul. It is the story of creation, of a grand and eloquent design beyond my abilities to imagine or understand. Nothing stands alone. All is bound together in balance, stretching back to a beginning and forward to a destiny, calling me to a meeting with the Maker of it all, the Giver of life. I am and I see and I hear and I appreciate and I feel and I think and I move and I imagine and I create and I believe and I love, because He gave me life for love with Him forever.

In the summer, I lie in the fields looking up at the sky, taking in the warmth with a potpourri of fragrances. I pretend the ground is like a ceiling that mysteriously holds and comforts my body above the infinite vastness of space. Blueberry vines surround me and cradle my head, alive with insects, each with a message, a purpose, and a community. I hear provision. The sun, the rain, the air, and the decomposing organic matter all give the vines what they need to spread roots. Leaves grow to collect energy, and the stems bear remarkably sturdy, nutritious, and delicious fruit. Seeds promise a future of life-sustaining food for insects, birds, animals, and people. The fields ask me to provide, to care for them gently, with reverence. They guide me to help, and they pray I will not harm. In the midst of the provision is the Provider, the Source—giving all that is needed to His beloved, for love's sake.

In the fall, the leaves of the blueberry vines turn scarlet red. Like a flaming carpet, they cover the fields. I sit in their midst and hear a celebration of completion. The plants have come to the end of another cycle of life, another link in an unbroken chain of life. They have had their day in the sun. They have done well. They have fulfilled their purpose, and so they joyfully rest in peaceful acceptance of the grand design. As this season passes for the cold and darkness of winter, I hear the sounds of sacrifice and surrender.

Gusts of wind sweep over the fields, and the leaves shimmer and shake, speaking their last words before leaving the vines for the bed of the field. They give all they have back to whence they have come, grateful and hopeful for the future. At the moment each leaf breaks free of the vine, I can hear the soft love songs of trust in the Maker and His will.

In the winter, the fields sleep beneath a sea of snow, with wind sculpting soft flowing waves of white. Scattered islands of granite rise up, almost seeming to float in the glistening sunlight. The cold dry air warns me that I don't belong there. Yet, I walk atop this crusty frozen sea and stand still in silence from place to place, listening beyond and beneath me. The fields tell me, *challenges will come that may at times feel unbearable, but fear not. There is something within that is strong and wise that will find a way through.* This voice was a gift from a loving protector who knows all I need to make my way and the limits of what I can bear. I hear encouragement to live simply, with clarity about what is important and what is not. I am reminded that I am never alone and that together with others, we are forever in the midst of preparation for new growth. I am told to look within, as the secrets of the universe were planted there in my believing and loving soul.

Turning around, Jesus saw them following and asked, "What do you want?" (John 1:38)

Listening is an uncommon gift. It is a beautiful act of love. It requires strength, the ability to put aside completely the powerful pull of our ever-flowing desires and the noisy temptations of the world, and to give to another everything we have, the present moment of our being. Our attention is one of our most valuable resources. We have the choice to shift it about and place it wherever we like. It is the gateway to our awareness. We will take in whatever our attention is fixed upon, which will activate our perception, memory, thought, emotion, motive, and action, all in a seamlessly flowing experience. Of course, our attention can be withheld and used as yet another weapon of rejection. At any time, people may close the gate, and there is nothing we can do about it

Listening is much more than hearing what someone may say. True listening is the complete and unconditional giving of one's attention. It includes taking in what can be seen, touched, smelled, and tasted, what can be understood about another person's experience, and what can be felt empathically. Ultimately, it is knowing what another's desires are and what is important to them at that moment that they may need for their safety, health, and well-being of body, mind, and spirit. Listening is an active searching and discovering that is done together with another person. It is a deliberate and intentional act, in which we trust that the other is the only one who knows and can convey priceless information vital for loving. To listen, we must follow the other's guidance, learn her language as she shares and reveals her message. Only the other will know when we have listened. Only the other can affirm when we have "gotten it."

Listening requires a measure of courage and faith. It is a venture into the unknown. It could be risky, since we may not like what we hear. We may be afraid that what is important to another may exclude what is important to us. We may not see how we will get what we want or make our way in the world if we stop and listen to others. Listening may lead to conflict, as differences in opinion, emotions, values, and desires may come to light.

Generally, people desperately want other people to listen. Curiously, many are loath to listen, as if they will go without something vital they need. If we are not listening, we are alone. For people who have been neglected, have been abused, or who have not known true loving, being alone offers an illusion of safety and control. These are people whose experience in relationships has been unpredictably hurtful. They may not have been able to trust what they were hearing. They may have found disappointment and conflict when they tried telling others about what they wanted. Over time, a sense of helplessness may have grown in their relations with others, so that the only safe place they could find and the only place where they could feel they were in control was in their isolation. They make their way in the world by being either givers or takers.

Jesus showed us in His life that it is important to ask and find out what other people want, and it is important to tell others about our desires. As the living God, surely He knows well what we're wanting and would not need to ask us. Yet, over and over, He has asked, and He has shown us what perfect listening is like. He listened for the contents of people's hearts and their soulful yearnings. How unusual and profound it must have been to have experienced firsthand Jesus' listening. It would have been uncommonly safe, peaceful, and loving. Do you know He is listening to you now? And He wants to give you the great gift of His love, if you will listen to Him.

We could not have a greater inspiration and encouragement for listening than Jesus. He has taught us to listen with acceptance, respect, and openness to receive what others have to say, feel, and desire. Listening is actually a powerful way of developing relationships and people. It is affirming of people's value and worth. It makes possible the sharing of joys and burdens. It reassures us that we are not alone.

People who are shouting, or in other ways dramatically calling attention to themselves, may be trying to force people to listen because they have not been heard in the past and fear that no one is listening or that they do not matter. Casualties of rejection, these people, in their desperation, tragically alienate others who could listen. If we try to force people to listen, we invite defensiveness and reduce the likelihood of understanding. It is extraordinary that God, with infinite power, has never forced someone to listen. He has faithfully respected our free will.

Speakers have a message to send and a method for sending it. Directly or indirectly, all the contents of communication ultimately refer to desires. We may give people information about observations or describe ideas and thoughts that may seem to have no bearing on desires; however, this kind of information provides a context or background that will help give meaning to the desire embedded there. Sometimes people who are uneasy about openly expressing their desires will hint or give clues to their listeners about what they want by talking about what they see, hear, think, or feel. To listen well, we must listen for desires, which are the heart of the message. How the message is sent conveys critical desires people have for acceptance and respect, peace and safety, understanding, help, comfort, and love. A message delivered in an angry way may express, albeit poorly, all of these critical desires.

As listeners, we are naturally drawn to the emotion in communication. What people feel is a magnet for attention. When we see tears welling up in someone's eyes, we are moved instinctively to touch and comfort him. Likewise, we are mobilized to protect the fearful and help the frustrated. Emotions seem to be a simple, eloquent, universal, and powerful way of communicating critical desires; this communication method is rooted in our nature and apparent even at the beginning of life. There can be no doubt that the capacity to feel and the unconscious or natural ability to express emotion were deliberately designed and created by God. For each of us, our emotions comprise a sophisticated and elegant guidance system.

Aspects of our minds constantly monitor the needs of our bodies, minds, and spirits in the context of time and space. We hunger, thirst, tire, and feel pain. We experience ranges of temperature, skin sensitivities, balance, and orientation. We have hearing, taste, and smell sensitivities that can immediately call our attention to important desires and move us to act. The basic emotions of comfort and discomfort orient us to when desires have been satisfied and when they have not. The feeling of comfort is associated in memory with the way desires are satisfied, so that in the future when a similar desire occurs, memories of ways to obtain comfort will come to mind.

The feeling of discomfort calls our attention to the need or desire that is present and automatically activates problem-solving and memory centers in the brain to generate ideas for managing the desire. While the discomfort is not pleasant, it instantly alerts us that an important desire requires our attention. Imagine what would happen to human beings if the feeling of hunger were pleasurable. Pain reflexively activates protection and safety seeking.

The emotions of frustration, anger, sadness, and fear deserve special consideration. In the psychological and social realms, these are the four basic uncomfortable emotions. Virtually all the other uncomfortable emotions are variations of one of these basic emotions. Each of them calls attention to a unique class of desires. Frustration is a signal or alarm letting us know when we are at our limit. It is very useful to know when we do not know something or when everything we have tried to manage a desire has not worked. Frustration lets us know that it is important to interrupt what we're doing, calm down, and think about what we could do differently or get help from someone with knowledge and experience we need. Since we all have unlimited limitations, frustration can be a handy cue to spare ourselves misery and enable us to spend more time in creative, playful discovery or join together with others in a loving experience of learning. Frustration leads the way in the development of our potential and talents, and it builds mutually supportive relationships with an endlessly expanding number of people.

Anger is an emotion many people associate with destruction and hurt. It is often considered a "bad" feeling. Yet, like the other three basic uncomfortable feelings, the emotion is valid, and it is present for a good reason. It is what we do with the emotion that determines whether it is helpful or hurtful, loving or sinful. Anger can be used as a weapon to punish people who have not given us what we've wanted or to force people against their will to give us what we want. We can also turn anger against ourselves if we cannot take care of it with others; we do this by denying what we want and rejecting or shaming ourselves for feeling angry. These are obviously selfish and destructive ways of managing the desires underlying anger.

Anger can also be the catalyst for creativity and construction of character and loving relationships.

Jesus advised us to be "slow to anger." He did not condemn the emotion. He encouraged us to slow down, that we might remain calm, clearheaded, and able to see all of what is happening in us, around us, and between others and us. If we are slow, we are then deliberate, mindful, able to think with discernment, and able to appreciate both our choices and the likely consequences of those choices, so that we can act purposefully.

At the heart of anger is an important desire. Its importance fuels passion that can drive us to fight for our desires or flee in a desperate attempt to turn off the uncomfortable experience of anger, even at the cost of going without what we desire. This is our nature, since the biochemistry and neurology of anger drain blood from the brain to the muscles and shut down the prefrontal cortex, which is where we think. But this is not necessarily our destiny, if we are slow to anger.

The important desires underlying anger generally come in two forms. There are momentarily intense desires for comfort, whether in the body, the mind, or a relationship with another, where there is a barrier or obstacle in the way of gratification. There are omnipresent desires to be accepted, respected, understood, fulfilled, at peace, and loved by others that may be thwarted. If you want something real bad and can't have it, you will likely feel mad. The feeling can energize, cause a single-minded focus, and generate determination to overcome the obstacle. Unfortunately, when we take care of our anger alone, it usually makes a mess and escalates our conflict; no one wins. When we join together with others in a loving alliance, virtually all obstacles can be managed with abiding benefit for the relationship and everyone involved.

Anger is also a sensitive alarm that will let us know when we are being treated in unloving ways. When we realize we have been treated in conditionally accepting ways, anger will be stirred as we experience being used. Rejection instantly activates the anger alarm and may propel us toward fight or flight mode, unless we are slow to anger and skilled at relating in loving ways. Similarly, if we are treated disrespectfully or as adversaries or ignored and not heard or forced to give what another desires, the anger alarm will sound.

Like all the uncomfortable emotions, anger is telling us to stop what we are doing and give our undivided attention to what is happening. Anger tells us that there is a real or potential danger or threat, as well as gives us an opportunity to grow in the strength of loving and enrich a relationship. By first restoring our peace to think clearly about what we would like to see happen, and by conveying this message simply and peacefully in the form of a request, we invite a potential enemy to be an ally. Should she choose to proceed alone and deny this request, it is loving to insist she accept, respect, listen, and collaborate as a condition for continuing the interaction. Making a stand for a mutually loving resolution is beneficial to all and, at the very least, is an excellent way of taking care of oneself.

The emotion of sadness is associated with loss. Something important to us in some way is missing. Like the other uncomfortable emotions, sadness can be experienced in degrees of intensity, which roughly approximate the importance of the missing object. A modest degree of sadness may be felt if one were to lose a favored toy or the car keys. Losing a spouse or child as a result of illness or accident would be a profound and intense loss, generating painful, deep, and enduring sadness. The emotion calls attention to what is missing, and the intensity lets us know just how important the loss is to us. The emotion asks us to set aside other matters and devote ourselves to recovering the loss. The emotion quite naturally conveys to others in a powerful way our need for comfort, support, and help. Often in our sadness, tears will be shed, which helps remove toxins from the bloodstream that may be responsible for the painful aspect of sadness. Tears will stir others in empathy to join us and go through the sadness with us. Restoration comes through relationship. The resolution of sadness is loving.

When we are sad, the most profound comfort we can obtain is through the love of Jesus Christ. He came for us because the most important relationship of our lives was lost, the loving relationship with God, our Creator. This loss has been apparent in the world from the beginning of time and could not be more obvious in today's world. Anyone who is living without a loving relationship with the one true God intuitively knows something critical is missing and is apt to search unceasingly in this world, by his own acts, for a way to resolve this "existential" sadness. It is a search that is doomed and likely to deepen the sadness as time goes on. This will happen because the God of love is trying to get our attention through His Spirit in order to tell us that what we are doing is not working, so it would be worthwhile to try another way, especially His way.

What could be better in the midst of sadness than to have Jesus Christ with you, embracing you, comforting you, and faithfully joining you in restoring and recovering what is more important than anything? So great is His love that He has left the throne of heaven to be with you, feeling your sadness and pain, understanding perfectly, and offering pure and complete healing, love, and peace that surpasses all understanding. The people around us, no matter how faithful, will likely sooner or later disappoint or reject us, because they are human, with unlimited limitations and an essentially selfish nature. We can see, hear, and touch the people around us, but no one can enter our hearts or souls except Jesus, whom we cannot see, hear, or touch, at least during our lifetimes. If we turn to Jesus for comfort for our sadness, then the support we can obtain from others or give to others will be meaningful and emotionally fulfilling. We shall not lack if the people around us, in their limitations or misery of their own, fall short of offering comfort.

Fear is an uncomfortable emotion, calling attention to our need to enhance or secure our safety. It is a sensitive alarm activated by an aspect of our minds, which are constantly monitoring the status of our safety. The intensity of fear approximates the degree of threat, which may come in the form of risk of bodily harm; risk of rejection, loss of control, or loss of love; and the most profound risk of all, the risk of separation from God.

Naturally, fear has survival value. Threats to life or limb, real or imagined, will trigger a "fight or flight" response. In these moments, thinking is not necessary; in fact, the prefrontal cortex (the thinking center) in the brain is instantly shut down, and unconsciously powerful instincts take over.

As a twenty-year-old youth running ahead of the bulls in Pamplona, Spain, I had fallen over a runner who had stumbled as we approached the small entrance of the arena. At that moment, the crowd was electrified as the bulls entered the plaza that led to the entrance. In the chaos of this moment, many men fell over us in a frantic effort to avoid the danger of the approaching bulls. I was at the bottom of the pile in darkness, dazed and disoriented, with a great weight pressing me to the ground. In an instant, the bodies that were on top of me flew forward. There was light, and inches from my face, the hoof of a bull struck the ground like thunder, and was gone. In the next moment, on its own, my body rolled quickly over and over to hug the wall of a barricade outside the arena as the swarm of stampeding bulls and running men passed by. It took a minute or so to get my wits about me. When I began to comprehend what had just happened, I was flooded with fear, my body shivering and shaking as if I were bitterly cold. Later, it occurred to me that had I felt the fear at the time of the danger, I likely would have been frozen in place and in great peril. At the moment I needed to act to save my life, there was no thought. There was calm, and there was instinct, as if someone had taken over my body to protect me. How wonderful it is that we are made in this way!

> The Lord is my shepherd; I have everything I need.
> He lets me rest in fields of green grass and leads
> me to quiet pools of fresh water. He gives me new
> strength. He guides me in the right paths, bringing
> honor to His name. Psalm 23:1–3(NLT)

In situations where the risks are less serious or immediate, fear comes as a warning, asking us to stop and think about how we can proceed alone or with others more safely. One beautiful summer afternoon, I was hiking in Acadia National Park, near Bar Harbor, Maine. I was scaling a granite wall that was about fifteen feet high on the slope of a mountain. I was alone and well off the trail. As I was pulling myself up the wall and stepping to a new foothold, the grip of my left hand gave way, and for a moment I was dangling, with a drop of fifty feet below me and all my weight on the fingers of my right hand. Instantly, my feet and left hand sought places on the wall to support my weight. A flash of fear swept over me as I comprehended what could have happened. Then, as if someone was sending me a message, the idea came to mind to test the security of my hand and footholds before putting my weight on them. The rest of the passage was a safe one.

The way our minds work in the midst of fear provides a strong encouragement to turn to others when we face threats and need to establish safety. Children do this instinctively. More than adults, children immediately know when they are at the limit of their capability and spontaneously look for help. If help is not available to them, this can be highly traumatic. Still, even children have built into their minds astonishing mechanisms for coping. If the threat is coming from someone they trust, they can detach from that person and from their emotional experience while searching in their own beings for comfort. How comfortably children seek out help for safety says a great deal about how dependable and able caretakers have been at responding to children's fears.

If our genetic design for physical safety is to turn to others for help, even if the help comes from another dimension of ourselves not normally accessible, no wonder this also is our "instinct" when facing dangers of an emotional or spiritual nature, particularly rejection. The fear of being unwanted, unloved, or alone seems as potent as threats to our lives. In fact, those who believe they are unwanted, unloved, or alone are uniformly dangerous to others, themselves, or both. Just as physical threats come in a range of risks, rejections come in many shapes and sizes. We may be rejected by others, rejecting of ourselves, or rejecting of others and God. The rejection may be mild, as when the salt and pepper were not passed quickly enough or when we live a day without a moment of prayer; or, it may be severe, such as banishing others from our lives or deliberately turning away from God forever.

Rejections activate fear or anxiety. The mind God created is as sensitive to this danger as the body is sensitive to physical harm. Rejections isolate, and it is dangerous to be alone. Rejection-based fear is an alarm, calling our attention to the need to restore loving connections. We were meant to live together with God and others in love. Long-standing exposure to rejection in the absence of help from others will encourage detachment and learning to live without others in a loveless pursuit of selfish comfort and addiction. Over time, such people will become cold and hardened to the rejections from others and callous about using and abusing others for their whims. Yet, these people know no peace. They live profoundly empty and alone, restless and unfulfilled. Their fears are ignored and sealed over. They are buried while still alive. Deep down, they believe something is grossly wrong with them, which they have decided to accept because being alone, this belief is impossible to overcome. To protect themselves from the hurt of rejection, they construct a prison of no escape and place themselves in solitary confinement. And yet, at any moment, even these people have the choice to do something different. Their past is not an excuse. God, who is gracious, merciful, and forgiving calls them as long as they have life to surrender to love. The fear or anxiety associated with the belief in rejection is the Holy Spirit calling attention to our belief in a lie about our or others' importance. Fear truly is a gift from God. The fear lets us know that believing in rejection separates us from God and others, mobilizes us to seek Him and others for our spiritual safety, and motivates us to seek His and others' love to establish truth.

Listening to God, to others, and emotions is vital to knowing the desires of God, others, and ourselves. It is an act of loving to listen. Jesus showed us how to listen humbly, selflessly, with acceptance and empathy, and with an intent and focus to understand. He showed us how to listen deeply, to go beyond the words and nonverbal communication to the heart and soul of the message. He taught us listen first to God and then to others before trying to be heard. By listening to God and each other, we prepare the way for mutual giving and receiving of the fullest blessings of love.

CHAPTER 10

Desire

Delight thyself also in the Lord; and He shall give thee the desires of thine heart.

—Psalm 37:4 (KJV)

EVERY STRIDE you and the woman take is another step into a deepening and unfolding beauty. Everything around them is bathed in the soft, pure light. Gardens of brilliantly colored flowers and orchards of succulent fruits adorn the path, which is winding its way toward the horizon and the brilliant source of light. The air is fragrant with roses, orchids, lilies, impatiens and a multitude of other flowers, as if each unique aroma is dancing a ballet in the air for their delight. The gardens and the forest beyond them seem to be reaching for the light, which dazzles brilliantly everywhere in the blue heavens. Soothing breezes, sweeping over and through the woods, carry songs of joy, composing a tapestry of sound; water trickles over rocks, birds and insects sing for the love of it, and moments of sweet stillness and silence fall between these sounds.

As they absorb and enjoy the beauty around them, they are all the more astonished by the beauty within and between them, born of the light. There is a rich sense of freedom, never experienced before. They each are now at the center of the other's awareness and care. Finally, they are free from themselves, less important than the other. It is exhilarating. They speak with gentleness and reverence; they listen faithfully and gratefully as they walk in the beauty, recalling where they had been, anticipating where they would be, and sharing a profound awe to be in the light. As if walking in a house of mirrors, where images are endlessly reflecting, the indescribable joys of heartfelt giving and soul-satisfying receiving are multiplying exponentially with each passing moment. To know the other's desires before knowing the self's desires; to be lovingly moving to serve as the fulfillment of being; to receive what is right, good, and true in radiant kindness; and to be one with the other are each a precious gem of joy, a blessing of the light.

The woman and you now feel a natural openness to reveal the river of desires flowing within them. Their memories of selfishness and conflict are fading away. Their understanding grows that revealing their desires is important for others, so that they may know what and how to give in order to complete a loving experience with another. Giving their desires to each other is another act of love. As they receive each other's desires, a healing forgiveness fills their spirits. The desire of all desires that rises up from their souls is to go to the source of the light. Together, they sing and dance joyfully in the beauty and love on the way to the horizon of light.

BLUEBERRIES, LIKE all living things, endlessly desire. There is a temperature they prefer during each season of the year, along with moderate winds and a certain amount of water and sunshine. There is a soil with nutrients of different sorts and an acidic pH they need to thrive. Without pollinators, their cycle of life would end. They need protection from blight and certain insects. Weeding helps to reduce competition for resources. Periodically, a traumatic yet rejuvenating fire strengthens roots, manages disease, and stimulates the production of fruit. Blueberries have their own unique language and method of expressing desire. At times, I admit it would be nice if they spoke English. They ask us to watch them closely in context with the seasons, weather, and constantly changing ecosystem of flora and fauna. The vines speak to us with their size and sturdiness; the thickness, shape, and color of their leaves and stems; the abundance of flowers in spring; the expanse and density of their root carpet; and, of course, the number, size, health, and sweetness of the blueberries on each vine. Blueberries can be remarkably forgiving if their desires are not fulfilled. They sacrifice, adjust, and find a way to survive with what they receive. If they are severely deprived, they will relentlessly try to recover. When Theresa and I appreciate their desires and respond well, they may bless us with abundance. But humbly we admit that what is beyond our control is vast and in the hands of the Divine Blueberry Grower, who has faithfully cared for the fields for millennia—indeed, from the beginning.

IN LATE July, 1998, I took a seat in the Alamo Theatre in Bucksport, Maine, having just finished arranging Gretchen's paintings, photographs, and collages for a final exhibition of the art of her life. In a few minutes, the doors to the theater would be opened, and we would have a brief ceremony to celebrate the occasion. One last deep emotional wave of grief swept through me. Tears filled my eyes as I felt the full measure of loving we had shared. The wave ran its course, carrying me to the shore of resolution. I had found a good place to preserve my loving experience with Gretchen and could let go of everything else. I was filled with gratefulness. I envisioned that the rest of my life would be dedicated to loving. At that moment, I was taken by surprise. From my soul, there came a pure encouragement to love again.

The exhibition was a joyous occasion. Over the period of a month, hundreds of people would visit and be moved by the emotional power of Gretchen's art. It reflected the hurt that comes in life and the healing power of love. As I stepped out of the theater into the noonday sun, a community festival was in full bloom along the harbor and in the streets. For some reason, the sun seemed more radiant, the sky more blue, and the air fresher. I crossed the street and went down to the harbor to take in the exhibits of artists, musicians, crafts, commercial and educational displays, and appetizing treats. It was a feast for the senses and a bustling, jovial gathering of people of all ages. I slipped into a childlike openness to enjoying it all, greeting and exchanging pleasantries of the day with acquaintances and friends. Suddenly, another momentous surprise overcame me. My eyes met the eyes of Theresa.

After her husband had divorced her, Theresa lived with her children for a while in Fort Worth, Texas, before deciding to return to Maine, where she had grown up with her family. She took up residence with her mother and father, devoted herself to her children, and entrusted her heart with her new husband, Jesus Christ. She was a faithful and devoted wife to Jesus. She spoke with Him throughout the day and shared everything. She joyfully sought His pleasure, comfort, and advice. As the years went by, she asked Him to bring one man, one good, God-loving man He could bless to be with her forever. She did not trust and had no patience for dating. She wished to forgo the oftentimes confusing and risky process of finding and getting to know a potential mate. She trusted Jesus would bring her together with the perfect man as an expression of His love for her, if it would be His will. She would wait and accept His choice.

When our eyes met, it was by the loving hand of God. How gently and gracefully He brought us to one another, knowing the desires of our hearts. Thereafter, when I would pick my children up after work, I was moved to linger for conversation, which soon became the highlight of our days. On a beautiful fall morning, I invited Theresa to walk with me through the woods at Highland. For a while, we agreed to walk in silence, and then we opened the doors of our hearts. At the walk's end we shared a kiss. In the days and weeks that followed, we spent time together with our children and with Theresa's mother and father. It was a sharing of the people who were most important to each of us, with Theresa and me together in their midst. I could not say this was a plan; it was just the way our relationship unfolded. When I asked Theresa if my sons and I might go with her and her family to church, it was a touching answered prayer. She had known shortly after meeting Gretchen and me that we did not attend church. She knew the loving relationship she desired would not be possible unless the foundation was a loving relationship with Jesus. She had not revealed this to me, but she had been praying for me, and for us.

In the Bible, when Martha asks Jesus to raise Lazarus from death, Jesus responds, "I know that even now God will give you whatever you ask." John 11:22(NLT)

Each of us, as we live and breathe, is standing in a river of desires. They flow along endlessly. Most desires are trivial and frequently overlooked, such as a desire to shift posture to a more comfortable position, to look in a different direction to satisfy a momentary curiosity, or to listen to what someone may be saying to us. If we were asked to describe our desires, these sorts of desires would not likely be mentioned. They are the sort of desires we unconsciously address the moment we are aware of them. These are a class of desires rooted in sensation and oriented toward momentary comfort. Our brains seem to be wired to seek out comfortable sensations and, of course, the brain uses the senses to gather important information that will be useful in fulfilling other desires.

Desires arise from our bodies for air, food, drink, warmth or coolness, rest or sleep, elimination, and so on. An aspect of our minds is constantly monitoring the body for what it needs to function properly. Our bodies can communicate with our minds to inform and activate us to acquire what is needed. The longer any need is unfulfilled, the more intensely the body will convey discomfort. When we take action to satisfy the desire, the body rewards us with comfort. If we overdo it, the body will let us know by creating discomfort. The most potent desire in this class is the desire for survival. It is the most basic desire, which easily overrides all other desires in priority. It is a desire that activates immediate, unconsciously driven action to preserve life. If the threat to survival is not immediate but imminent, this desire may wash out other values and orient all decision making and action for security. Curiously, a choice will remain to accept the risk of death for the sake of love, but the flesh will resist this choice. Remember Jesus in the Garden of Gethsemane when He asked His Father, "… if it is possible, let this cup pass from Me; nevertheless, not as I will, but as you will." Matthew 26: 39 (NKJV)

The mind has its own set of desires. It seeks to explore, experiment, learn, and create. It wants problems solved, goals achieved, resolution, and closure. It also desires peace, calm or excitement, comfort and challenge, and emotional well-being. In a similar way, the body communicates with the mind, so the mind can speak to itself by way of comfort and discomfort. Boredom can launch exploration. Frustration can spark creativity. Anxiety may stimulate planning, and so on. Like the body, if the mind overindulges its desires, there will be discomfort in the form of perceptions, such as, "Is that all there is?" or an unquenchable craving for more. Our minds seem to have been made to work like compasses orienting us to live, grow, be healthy, and love.

Another set of desires arises from our social experience. We desire connection with others, deep bonds and attachments that can provide for our survival. Our bonds make exchanges of support possible; for example, nurturing, guidance, practical help, and teamwork all result from deep interpersonal connections. We desire safe, trusting, and dependable relations with others. We desire acceptance, respect, peace, understanding, and love. If any of these desires is unfulfilled, there will be an uncomfortable restlessness, yearning, sadness, or emptiness calling attention to what is missing. When these desires are fulfilled, there will be a measure of peace and joy.

Spiritually, there is only one desire—to be united forever in a loving relationship with God. We can get a glimpse of this desire in our fantasies of happiness, of being forever young, of being loved perfectly, and of living forever. It seems to be a desire like survival that is ever present, behind the scenes, influencing profoundly the way we conduct our lives. It is there every time we make a choice. We may choose to live without God and instead live for ourselves. If we do, this choice contaminates the pool of our desires, sets us adrift alone in a carnal world that is a prison of insatiable appetites. If we choose to live with God, for Him, our desires can become stepping-stones to fulfillment in this life and in eternity. This choice, fervently and faithfully made, will enlighten all other choices. From that moment on, we shall have the choice, wherever we may be, whatever may be happening, to act in a way that would increase and demonstrate our love of God and others as we respond to the desire of the moment. The other two choices offer quite a contrast. Living for ourselves is soulless, harmful, and dangerous. Living for love without God is fleeting, uncertain, and limited, with loss assured. Each time we make a choice, we will experience immediate spiritual feedback. Either we shall have peace that is deep and satisfying; peace that is fleeting; or no peace at all.

Just as our bodies, minds, and spirits are one, the desires of each aspect of our beings have intimate relationships with each other. They are all present for good reason. They are valid but potentially helpful or harmful, depending upon what we do about them. Together they are guiding us to health, happiness, love, and eternal life. When we choose to indulge one desire in isolation from the desires of other aspects of our beings, we will bring harm to our bodies, minds, and relationships with people or with God. Pleasuring our bodies without regard for anything else will lead to disease and death, a mind full of deception, shallow and conflicted relationships, and eternity without God. The same would be inevitably true if a person were to indulge only the desires of her mind or the desires arising from relationships. Only attending to the spiritual desire would, as a matter of course, involve balanced and responsible management of all other desires.

It is God's desire that we would be with Him, believe in Him, and love Him. When we choose to give God what He desires, we can then look on our desires as opportunities to act in ways that would be loving to God and others. Increasingly, our lives become an act of praise for God, His creation, His salvation through Jesus Christ, the indwelling of His Spirit, His gift of life as one of His children, and His promise of eternal love. We shall live gratefully and thoughtfully, making sure as many of the choices we make as possible will please Him and conform to His desires or will for us. We will care well for the body He has given to each of us, a self-contained replica of the cosmos He created and a literal reminder that we are one part of the body of Christ. We will develop the minds and talents we were given to learn about Him and His creation and to celebrate and show the world just how glorious He is and how profound is His love. We will treat and love others as He has loved us.

Ultimately, the purpose of our desires is to draw us into loving God and others. Our deepest desire is to love. As we all know, this can be hard to believe when we look at the state of the world or the state of our own lives. In isolation from others, our desires will draw us into conflict with others. If we cannot work together to resolve conflicts, then we will be working against each other, and all will lose. For this reason, desires for most people are risky to reveal. As children, we naturally and spontaneously expressed desires, unaware that others were busy pursuing desires of their own. Some of the time, people would be pleased and even enjoy giving children what they wanted, but at other times they would be annoyed or rejecting. As children grow up, they learn that revealing their desires is a gamble. Sometimes they win and obtain what they want, but frequently conflicts and rejection result. Since desires continue to flow endlessly, children gradually learn ways of hiding desires from others.

By adolescence, a common response to the question "What do you want?" is "I don't know." This is a safe answer. Sometimes, what is desired is known; however, adolescents make a forecast that revealing their desires either would not result in acquiring them or could spark conflict and rejection. A good deal of the time when people say, "I don't know," their minds are truly blank. Having had too much conflict and rejection, the mind unconsciously conceals desires, even from oneself, all for the sake of safety. The desires may surface later when the person is alone and able to consider different ways he can obtain what he wants without anyone interfering. Without acceptance, respect, and peace, there will be no connection or trust—only isolation, where desires grow in importance, even surpassing the value of others.

Another cautious response to the question "What do you want?" is a vague, abstract, or general expression of desire, such as, "I want you to be nice to me," or "I want you to be my friend." These answers attempt to sidestep conflict and rejection by appealing to universally accepted values. Who could be against being nice or friendly? These expressions of desire subtly test to see if there is acceptance, and they put pressure on anyone who may be reluctant to accept. If you will be nice or friendly, then maybe it will be safe to reveal exactly what is desired, and chances are good that you will provide what is desired to maintain the status of being a nice or friendly person. Vague expressions of desire are delivered in a conditionally accepting and rejecting package.

The listener to vague expressions of desire is apt to be confused and defensive. She must guess or use imagination to understand exactly what is desired, with a likelihood of being wrong. After all, no matter how well we know a person, how could we correctly guess exactly what he wants in any given moment? The general expression of desire is like a request to sign a blank check. To be nice or friendly not only applies to the present moment but also to countless and unforeseen situations in the future. The listener may wonder what she may be getting herself into or become suspicious of being set up for manipulation. The listener will also stand accused, since it is implied that she is not nice or friendly. The listener will recall instances when she was nice or friendly. The listener will resent being judged and pressured to provide what is desired, or face rejection. The ingredients for adversarial conflict will be in place. The interaction will no longer be about fulfilling desires but rather about self-preservation.

A third, very common defensive answer to the question of what you want, is blunt, sometimes vague statements about what a person does not want. "Leave me alone," "Stop," "Don't," "I hate it when you …" and so on. These messages, often delivered in harsh emotional tones with rejecting nonverbal communication, invite resistance, or even a fight. Some people who describe what they want this way are showing some of their battle scars from past conflicts. They may assume other people care little for them or what they want or that other people, selfishly pursuing their own desires, will interfere or stop them from obtaining what they may want. They are alone and self-absorbed, with weak connections to others by default because they have had too many relational experiences based on conditional acceptance and rejection. They predict their best chance to obtain what they want is to stop others, by force or implied threat, from interfering. There are others who may communicate their desires this way in situations in which they are frustrated. When being accepting, respectful, and peaceful has not resulted in acquiring what was desired, we are apt, in desperation, to attack what seems to be the obstacle. There are also urgent situations in which safety may be in question, so there is no time for explanation or dialog. Then, negative expressions of desire are meant to grab others' attention and simply convey critical information for their welfare.

The problem with negative expressions of desire is twofold. It will leave the listener wondering what is desired, and it invites resistance. If we tell people what we don't want, how are they to know what we do want? Think of the contrast of appreciation when looking at a photographic negative compared to a colored print. When people are told to stop or not do something, the image in their minds at that moment may be clear about what not to do; however, the image for what they could do instead is missing. These images are an important precursor for action. If the listener were willing to help, he is left without a map or plan for how to help. Lacking a clear understanding of what is desired will weaken the connection between people and will more likely result in unfulfilled desires and/or continuing interference. We are all familiar with the experience of having desires that others simply don't understand. We all know the painful frustration and helplessness of wanting to help someone when we do not know exactly what she wants. Negative expressions of desire are a form of communication that separate people from one another and fuel misunderstanding and conflict.

When we tell people what we don't want, we rivet their attention and imagination on what we do not want to happen and, at the same moment, encourage their opposition. If I respectfully and peacefully say to you, "Don't think of a pink elephant," what happens? For most people, the image of a pink elephant immediately comes to mind. It seems our minds are constantly vigilant and protective of our free will or choice. If someone comes along and tells us not to do something, he is crossing a boundary, and our minds are apt to react automatically, as if to say, "Wait a minute. You can't tell me what to think. That's my choice. Here's your pink elephant." When we tell someone not to do something, we are trying to forcefully set aside whatever their desire may be at the moment and thus, by example, proposing it would be all right for them to do the same thing to us. Our unconscious minds, which cannot distinguish between real and imagined threats, instantly react as if an attack on our free will is underway. Once again, the interaction will then leave the field of fulfilling desires and move to the level of wondering who is controlling whom.

It is profoundly sad that openly, simply, honestly telling each other exactly what we want at any given moment has become both rare and risky. When we hold back expressing this precious information, we impose isolation on ourselves and pass up an opportunity for a loving experience. People do this because the rejections they have experienced in the past came when they revealed what they wanted. The illusion developed that safety depended upon keeping this information secret. This great deception orchestrated by the master of rejection has turned our relational experience upside down. What is good—i.e., describing to each other specifically what we desire—has become bad; and what is bad—i.e., concealing what we desire from others—has become good. The net effect of all of this has been to weaken loving on a grand scale, while propagating selfishness and conflict.

Jesus' exemplary life boldly encourages us to be keenly interested in the desires of others and to simply express our own desires. The human experience of loving depends upon it. When desires are unknown or below the level of awareness, let us stand still in the midst of unconditional acceptance, respect, and peace. Then wait and trust that what is important will come to mind, so it can be spoken and shared. When desires are vague, abstract, or general, let us consider or visualize exactly what we want to see happen. If a photograph could be taken of the moment desire would be fulfilled, let us describe to others what we would see happening in the picture. When desires are expressed in negative forms, let us acknowledge what is not desired and then go forward together to explore what would be desired instead. When we are equipped with the great love of God, we have nothing to fear. He desires that we love Him with all of our being. By fulfilling His desire, our beings are fulfilled. He desires to love us beyond our wildest dreams. How much of His love we receive depends upon the depth and breadth of our love for Him. When we spend our time "loving" ourselves and what the world offers us, we miss the great love He is offering. With Him, we can go boldly into the world loving others, seeking the desires of others' hearts, and sharing our own, all for His glory.

CHAPTER 11

Fulfillment

I tell you the truth, the son can do nothing by himself; he can do only what he sees the Father doing, because whatever the father does the son also does. For the Father loves the Son and shows him all he does.

—John 5:19

Blessed be God who comforteth us in all our tribulation, that we may be able to comfort them which are in any trouble, by the comfort wherewith we ourselves are comforted of God.

—2 Corinthians 1:3,4 (KJV)

THERESA AND I began the blueberry harvest of 2004 with some anxiety. In January and the beginning of February, a deep freeze settled over coastal Maine, with biting winds and temperatures near zero for a three-week period, without much in the way of snow cover. These conditions are associated with "winterkill," a drastic stress on the blueberry plants that results in the plants channeling energies normally given to flowering and fruit bearing to strengthening roots, vines, stems, and leaves. The spring was unusually cool, overcast, and wet, discouraging pollination. The summer also was unusually cool, overcast, and rainy. When we walked around the edges of the field during the spring and summer, the blueberries were scattered and sparse. Theresa and I drew up a harvest plan; instead of selling to supermarkets, our largest customers, we decided to conserve what blueberries we had for our private customers, thus cutting back our production costs to a minimum. Our fellow blueberry growers were expecting harvests that were below normal production by between thirty-five and fifty percent. Some growers, to cut their losses, would not even harvest what they had.

Before our raking crew went into the fields, I laid out boundaries of eight-foot wide rows or "ricks" with large spools of kite string. Stringing the field insures an orderly and thorough harvest, as each raker is assigned one rick at a time. As I walked the fields, laying down the string, I could hardly believe my eyes. They were filled abundantly with blueberries—many of them were smaller than usual, but there were many more than expected that were plump and juicy. Their taste was sweet and sublime. There was no other way to explain it. This harvest was a blessing from God.

I felt a growing awe and wonder as I reverently walked back and forth across the field, string spinning off the spool. The fruit at my feet was the product of a dazzling and complex array of natural and biological forces beyond understanding that somehow were working together with extraordinary harmony and balance. The weather, the soil, the flora, and the fauna, each a system of systems with webs of interdependence, share a secret recipe for the Maine wild blueberry. How could this be an accident? The blueberry, with its power to prevent cancer and Alzheimer's disease; to control high blood pressure, cholesterol, and diabetes; and to prolong and enhance the quality of life, could only be a gift from God, heralding His unimaginable glory.

On August 9, Theresa, the harvest leader, assembled a crew of Christian youth to rake the fields and prepare the blueberries for market. She began with a devotion to God, reading from the Bible and praying for His blessing of protection, strength, and love for the work to come. From sunrise to sundown over the course of the following three weeks, nearly nine tons of organic blueberries were taken from the fields, cleaned, packaged, and cooled or frozen fresh within hours of leaving the vines. Customers came to the farm in a stream that matched the flow of the berries from the field. Theresa, our family, and the young people worked together as one, sharing a sense that God was with us. The work was long and difficult, but joyous. We left on the floor of the fields many blueberries for seed and as an offering for what we had taken. We gave praise and thanks to God.

JUST AS drops of rain make their way to a stream, and the stream flows into a river that winds its way to the sea, the woman and you walking in the light join together with an ever-growing number of people of all ages, making their way to the brilliant light at the horizon. Myriads of paths converge into thoroughfares, like capillaries into veins, conveying a flow of people like blood to the heart. Exuberant joy fills the air as the you and woman share mutual greetings with others, sweetly filled with acceptance, peace, and love. They tell each other inspiring stories about finding the light and how they were transformed. Their bonds with one another deepen as they journey on, and the light glows more brightly in them. Time vanishes. Everyone walks energetically in delight, with excited anticipation of reaching the horizon. How far and how quickly they travel does not matter. The beauty surrounding them and flowing from them is endlessly fascinating.

The thoroughfares ascend an impressive and mighty mountain, filling with people as they approach the summit where the passages come together. The top of the mountain is crowned with countless shafts of glistening white light that reaches into the heavens and bathes all in radiant love, peace, and truth. Over the top of the mountain, the river of people slowly flows in silence where the sounds of awe, wonder, and joy were unbridled just moments before. A few steps from the crest, you and the woman look into each other's eyes, smile, and take the other's hand before turning their gazes to the horizon from the top of the mountain.

Instantly, the light passes through them, fills them, purifies them, and completes them. The light's brilliance is momentarily overwhelming and blinding. Every molecule of their beings is illuminated. They become one with the light. Their empty hands join hands with others, and the light flows through them, connecting each with all others, as one body, one heart, and one spirit. Each unique soul is brilliantly refined, perfectly balanced, and tuned to give, receive, and share infinite and eternal love. In that moment, each one is alone in communion with the light and anointed with mercy, forgiveness, and love. It is simply known that never again would they be separate from the light or loving. They are a new creation in the light.

From the mountaintop, they behold a plateau and a golden city, stretching out as far as they can see. The light emanates from the heart of the city. The great thoroughfare of people is making their way to the city, singing together joyously of praise and thanksgiving for the light. The woman and the man soon enter the incredible city of beauty. Everywhere about them are golden palaces, each one utterly unique, adorned brilliantly with jewels of dazzling color and embraced by beautiful gardens. Through grand crystal windows there can be seen the great light glowing richly. Beyond what their senses can take in, there is a deeper, powerful, indescribable beauty that is filling their hearts and spirits to overflowing. It is the love of the light.

The love is calling them to the heart of the great city. They are drawn to a pure river of life and compelled to follow it to its source. On either side of the river, there is a tree of life, bearing twelve fruits and leaves for the healing of nations. Beyond, the great light and the river meet. As the you and woman approach the holy place, where life and love come together, they fall on their faces, humbled and overwhelmed. A soft voice speaks to them inside their hearts, "Come, be with Me forever." They stand in truth and walk joyously into the water and light, becoming one with the light, beaming endlessly through the darkness.

The city had no need of the sun or of the moon
to shine in it, for the glory of God illuminated it.
The Lamb is its light. Revelation 21: 23 (KJV)

ONE STILL, clear December night I stood with Theresa in the moonlight by the lighthouse at the mouth of the Penobscot River in Stockton Springs. I held her face in my hands as she embraced me. We looked into each other's soul. Our pasts and future met in the moment we kissed before God and gave each other our lives. We both felt an unprecedented certainty that the ordeals and loves of our lives had brought us to this moment of destiny by the hand of a faithful and loving God. On the last day of winter, before family and God, we were married at Highland. We planned the ceremony together and celebrated the formation of one family with our five children. Together, we dedicated Highland, the blueberry fields and surrounding woods, as a sanctuary and retreat for the encouragement of loving God and others. A Bible study that began at Highland in the fall of 1999 with Norman Labonte, an elder of Calvary Chapel in Bangor, became Safe Harbor Church when we ran out of space and found an empty church looking for a congregation in Searsport, a neighboring town on the coast of Maine. Loving became our passion by the grace of God.

The little boy who left home searching for love was at last blessed. The scientist who wanted to understand the essence of healthy relationships was enlightened. The husband, who lived through the darkness with Gretchen to stand briefly in the beautiful light of love, was fulfilled. The time had come for loving as a way of life, joining with God, each other, and everyone our lives would touch.

BEFORE TIME and the beginning of our lives, God loved us. He knew what we would do in our lives. He knew all about our selfishness and who we would hurt and how. He knew we would turn away, forget Him, and even reject Him, but He created us anyway. Despite our limited ability to understand the purpose and meaning of life, and our ungratefulness, He would sacrifice Himself, His only Son, to die in our place, so that we could be with Him in loving, forever. Could there be any greater demonstration of unconditional acceptance? Through the ages, God has been given every reason to reject humankind. The list of abominations is endless. In our own lives, we could not count all the selfish acts that are an affront to God and others. Yet, He has not rejected us, but with authority and truth He has forcefully rejected rejection. God, the infinite being without limitations, accepts each of us, beings with infinite limitations. Shouldn't we treat each other the way He treats us?

Each of us has the revered and respected position of being one of His children. This extraordinary gift of heritage is freely given to us, undeserved. He provides a relationship of complete peace and safety, inviting us to enjoy, live, and celebrate love with Him. These dimensions of His love merely set the stage for communion with Him. He delights in sharing with us the passions and desires of His heart and seeks to know ours. Forever His will has been to form a loving oneness with us, where we joyfully give our all to Him while He blesses us beyond our wildest dreams.

We are brothers and sisters in the royal family of the King of kings. In His love for all of us, it has been His design and intention that our relationships with each other would be purely loving. As recipients of His unconditional love, God encourages us to accept others—and Him, our Creator and Redeemer—with unconditional love. Thanks to His great wisdom, it immediately benefits and blesses us to give acceptance to others, just as this priceless gift is a blessing to others. We will experience a measure of peace and joy in giving so valuable a gift. We will begin a loving experience and, by our example, invite others to return the same gift to us, so that they will experience the same peace and joy. Acceptance, like each of the other six attitudes of the heart and acts of loving described in this book, is a shield of protection in our dealings with people who may be lost. Offering acceptance to someone who may be rejecting is precisely what Jesus taught in "turning the other cheek". Acceptance can dismiss the rejecting act and at the same time invite the one who is lost to join us. If he turns down the invitation, we might, as God treats us, ask him to let us know if he changes his mind. Making a stand for mutual acceptance is what God offers all of us.

When we appreciate that the value and worth of all God's children has been established and secured by God Himself, not by any status of birth, wealth, or power, then it becomes obvious that we are all entitled to profound respect from one another. Knowing God respects us, there can be no excuse or exception for respecting each other. This is the basis for treating others the way we would like to be treated. Imagine what the world would be like if we all treated each other like the royalty we are. Respect must be given without condition. It does not matter whether we are given respect or whether it is earned or deserved on the basis of others' actions. Like acceptance, respect is freely given as an invitation to loving. Respect protects the giver from rejection. Respect leads the lost from the darkness into the light. Respect blesses the giver and the receiver with a bond, freeing them from isolation. Respect grows trust and caring.

> Jesus said, "Peace, I leave with you, My peace I give to you; not as the world gives do I give to you. Let not your heart be troubled, neither let it be afraid." John 14:27

In our loving relationship with God, we are given peace—the deepest, strongest, and most complete and satisfying peace there is. With His peace, we are grounded, utterly safe, and able to live truly. With His peace, we can be fearless in our relationships with others. Rejection cannot hurt us. Our peace with Him can be contagious and put others at ease. Our peace shows others they have nothing to fear from us. They can lay their defenses down and be themselves. Our peace encourages peace in others. It was God's design that our relationships with others would be peaceful. If we are actively seeking or making peace, it will be difficult for others to refuse. In loving relationships, where there is an insistence upon peace, everyone will be a peacemaker. Peace can be offered to those with hurtful intentions. The hurtful will be turned away with peace and encouraged to return for forgiveness in peace.

When I was undergoing training as a medical corpsman in the Army, one night before lights-out, two big and strong platoon mates I did not know came to my locker, and in a loud voice one of them said, "We want to beat you up." Without saying a word I stepped out into the open middle of the barracks and faced the two men. I said to them so all could hear, "O.K., you want to beat me up. Before you get started I want to say just one thing. I will not defend myself. Go ahead and beat me up." The men seemed stunned and confused. It certainly was not what they were expecting. Without saying a word, the men backed away and returned to their bunks. There was peace between us for the remainder of the training. Looking back, I believe this was a moment when the Holy Spirit protected me.

When we deliberately accept others unconditionally, respect them, and make peace, and when we insist that others do the same as the only condition for relationship, we set the stage for fulfilling communion with others. We can and we must make a stand for loving, which is mutually enriching.

Communion involves communication and collaboration. In the Great Commandment, God tells us what is important above all else. He desires our love and love for others. What He desires is enormously beneficial for us and a blessing for Him. How it would help us if our desires were beneficial for others as well as ourselves! This guideline would cleanly separate selfish desires that ultimately would harm us from healthy desires that would grow us. God has simply, purely, and relentlessly expressed His desires to us throughout the Bible, in the life and teachings of Jesus Christ, and by the powerful guidance of the Holy Spirit in each of our lives.

Love Him and others. God has shown us by His example that it is important to express our desires directly and truly to others in ways they can understand. Even more important is seeking His and others' desires or will. At any given moment, what is important to God, to you, and to others? It is vital to share this precious information with one another to further the loving experience. With a mutual understanding of present desires, the stage is set for the final act, collaboration.

Every moment we have a fundamental choice to either pursue our desires alone or together with others in loving harmony. Despite our created destiny for loving, it is our nature to go it alone. Our bodies communicate with our minds in profound and intricate ways. Our desires do not simply materialize by chance. What we experience as a desire is the result of ongoing monitoring, below the level of awareness, of our physical, psychological, social, and spiritual needs. Our desires are given priority in our consciousness. As they surface, instantly other regions of the brain are activated for consideration of how to manage the desires. The brain relies on neurological structures, which automatically drive a problem-solving process of considering options and potential consequences for acting on any option. Like our breathing, these functions are also under our conscious control so that we may use them deliberately. In a split second, the brain also searches memories of experience that could be relevant for the management of a present desire. If we are reflective and receptive, the brain will continue searching and providing ideas we could use to take care of a desire. These ideas almost always fit us and seem better than the ideas others may give us, because they come from our own unique experience. In the same way the body is predisposed to reject a healthy organ transplanted into our bodies, even though tissues are carefully matched, our minds are biased to accept our own ideas over very good ideas that may come from others. All of this is clearly demonstrated by children who, for the most part, are grounded in their own experience with limited awareness of the experience of others. The saving grace for many children is that they intuitively know that there is a great deal they do not know, so they are open and, indeed, often interested in others' ideas or guidance.

As we mature, there are layers of psychological, social, and spiritual experience that encourage us to take care of our desires alone. Research on infants as young as two or three months has shown that if the parent is not responsive to their subtle or obvious expressions of desire, the infants will begin comforting themselves. Parents who notice and address the needs of infants inconsistently over time are unwittingly encouraging the development of foundational patterns for managing emotions and desires that are solitary. Certainly, to a degree, we all have experienced this breakdown of connection. Indeed, it is the forerunner of the fundamental human dilemma: when we are together with another, and each of us has our own river of desire, how do we deal with each other? No one can live unscathed or escape the predominant relating pattern of conditional acceptance and rejection, which is a solitary method of managing desire.

Last but not least, the forces of Satan seek to divide and conquer. God is His sworn enemy. He worships only himself. He does not have the power to directly hurt God; however, by destroying our love of God and others, Satan can capture and kill God's beloved children. No one does more to encourage selfishness and individual pursuit of happiness than Satan.

The only alternative for taking care of desire alone is taking care of our desires together. Like all other acts of love, this can only be done deliberately and purposefully—an act of our free will. Reverence must be given to each other's desires. Temptations to tamper with the desires of others must be resisted, because they lead down the path of rejection and adversarial conflict. The desires of individuals are equally important. It will not be good enough to take care of only one desire together. Loving demands a mutual giving and receiving. By the gift of free will, God ordained collaboration as the loving method of fulfilling desires. The collaboration between the Father, Jesus, and the Holy Spirit is so perfect that they are one. God invites us through prayer to lay our petitions before Him and to seek His will. By loving God with all our hearts, minds, souls, and strength, and loving others as ourselves, we receive His promise to bless us with our hearts' desires, and so much more. God will only hold back if, in His infinite wisdom, He knows a desire is harmful or that there is something better for us. In the same way, we are encouraged to join together with others to explore mutually beneficial ways of fulfilling desires, holding back only when loving dictates a desire will hurt or divide. Indeed, this is our responsibility.

After two or more people have shared their desires, it is time to put their hands, hearts, minds, and spirits together as they look for ways to address the desires, not stopping until each one is fulfilled. This process is itself a fulfillment of loving. It is a giving of oneself completely to another, deliberately setting aside selfish interests. Of course, we mutually share ideas for how one's own desire may be met; however, everyone places a greater value on finding mutually enriching ways of taking care of the desires of everyone involved. When we are engaged with unfamiliar people, or cautious about collaborating, it is loving to lead them in peace, respect, and acceptance. When we meet someone opposed to collaborating, it is loving to be firm and make a stand for collaborating as a condition for helping her obtain what she desires. After all, selfishness is encouraged and relationships are weakened if only one person's desires are met. Nothing is better than everyone winning, where everyone has the joy of both giving and receiving.

Pooling the experience of two or more people for taking care of desires is synergistic and can be great fun if done playfully. Everyone involved will have his own ideas. Hearing the ideas of others can spark the flow of other ideas that might not have surfaced. There can be streams of ideas, with each person sharing experiences for how she fulfills desires; new springs of ideas will then open by way of the ideas that are shared. Imagination and creativity are given free rein, while critical thinking is held in abeyance, so that anything goes. Even silly, absurd, funny, or outrageous ideas are welcomed because they may contain the seed for wonderful resolution. After a time when ideas are allowed to flow into the pool of acceptance—perhaps after a few moments, minutes, days, or even weeks—when there is a consensus to move on, joint consideration is given to the advantages and disadvantages of the available ideas. Forecasts are made about what would happen if the ideas were tried. An effort is made to find ideas or combinations of them that can fulfill everyone's desire and deepen loving in the process. Helping each other is a paramount value that permeates the experience of collaborating.

Collaboration balances the give-and-take in relationships. Not only is it the best way to fulfill desires, but it also is the best way for managing emotions, solving problems, and resolving conflict. The uncomfortable emotions of frustration, anger, sadness, and fear can be settled in a loving way through collaboration. Solving problems through collaboration allows the fluid exchange of knowledge, experience, skills, support, and power resources. Collaborating through conflict deepens trust, friendship, and intimacy. Learning, experimenting, and exploring are collaborative experiences. Collaboration is the pathway for every important human achievement, as well as for the mundane and practical, such as getting food on the table and clothing on our backs. Of course, not all collaboration may be considered good, since even gangsters and drug cartels appreciate the power of collaboration for getting things done. Truly loving collaboration will always involve at least three: self, other, and God.

The agencies and organizations we depend upon in our society for support, such as law enforcement, schools, hospitals, and churches, are systems of collaboration. Business and industrial organizations collaborate in bringing products to market and with customers in developing products. The quality of life in the community depends upon how well these various enterprises can collaborate with each other and the citizenry. Currency and our economic systems are based on collaborative principles. On a grander scale, society and even the nations of the world have their fates tied to collaboration. In human relationships, either we are working with people, or against them. We stand together, or alone. We love and benefit each other, or we hurt each other with our selfishness.

The body, mind, spirit, and soul collaborate to live in the world and prepare for eternity. Friendship, marriage, parenting, family, community relationships, churches, and counseling relationships depend completely on the quality of collaboration to flourish. Our relationship with God is the ultimate fulfillment of collaboration.

CHAPTER TWELVE

Heaven on Earth

My goodness is nothing apart from you. You will show me the path of life; in your presence is fullness of joy; at your right hand are pleasures forevermore.

—Psalm 16:2b, 11 (NKJV)

THE RELATIONSHIPS between the Father, Jesus, and the Holy Spirit are eternal, with no beginning and no end. Relationships between God and people and among people were meant to work a certain way, according to His loving design. He is the originator, the source, and the designer of relationships. Like everything else He created, there is a purpose, a form, an elegant order and organization, and a method of operation for the way God intended relationships to work. It is all about Jesus, the light, and His invitation to love, which also has neither beginning nor end.

We neglect this truth at our peril. Without the foundation of a loving relationship with God, we will either live as if relationships don't matter in our selfish pursuit of happiness, or our shallow forays into loving of our own creation will collapse under the weight of expectation we place on others and ourselves in the context of our brief and finite mortality. The disappointment, hurt, and losses in relationships will sooner or later overshadow the fleeting joy and hope of human-made loving.

The tragedy of humankind is a direct result of the absence of a loving relationship with God. Looking at the state of the world, it is safe to say that the vast majority of people on the planet, including those who believe in God, live without an ongoing loving relationship with Him. Because so much of humankind has lived without loving God, they do not know it is missing, even though evidence abounds in the form of their existential malaise and "man's inhumanity to man."

With epic mercy and grace, God relentlessly pursues each and every one of us for a loving relationship with Him. He has made us so that when we accidentally stumble upon any of the truth of loving, we will instantly be rewarded with a taste of joy and peace. When we're off track, He will let us know that what we are doing is not working by allowing us feelings of emptiness, boredom, sorrow, pain, anger, and fear, all of which invite us to discover something different, the healing force of love. He is calling us to our purpose and destiny in concrete, obvious, and practical ways. With minds made to wonder and believe, it is inevitable to ask, who am I? Where did I come from? Why am I here? What is love? How did it become so important? Why is it elusive and mysterious? The questions lead us to God.

It is God's plan and will that we live loving Him and others every waking moment, wherever we may be. He has made His choice. We have a choice between heaven and hell, loving Him and others or "loving" ourselves. If everyone would try living each of these choices for a time and compare the quality of living that each lifestyle offers, it would not be long before all of us would embrace God and each other. Loving God is the foundation for all loving; He illuminates, inspires, fortifies, deepens, enriches, nurtures, and guides the loving in all human relationships.

Friendship

Aristotle considered friendship an art. The quality of our bond with our mothers and fathers, and our experience of relationships with siblings, extended family, neighbors, caretakers, and peers in community settings, all shape our attitudes and capacities for friendship during childhood. During adolescence, the importance of friendships rivals the importance of family as youth earnestly prepare for adulthood. In our youth, we are exposed to a great variety of friendships, most superficial and short-lived but important nonetheless for gaining experience in the art and for appreciating the kinds of friendships we desire.

Common sense tells us that friends are good medicine, an extremely important source of joy, comfort, support, help, and fun. Friendship has been a timeless remedy for loneliness, boredom, and ennui; a constant in the midst of the shifting sands of change; a strength in facing challenges and fears; a healing force for trauma, pain, and sorrow; a source of power for achievement; a catalyst for goodness in people; and a blessing of love.

The essence of friendship and loving are one and the same—a relationship between two people who treat each other the way they want to be treated. In friendship, there is mutual acceptance and respect, and collaborations for peace, understanding, and mutual help. Friendships in childhood are momentous for being our first steps into the wider social world beyond our families. At the beginning, play is the bridge and catalyst for friendship. In play, children discover it can be fun and interesting to explore curiosity and imagination together with others. There also will be challenges as desires and wills conflict. The exuberance of fun drives children to prevent and overcome conflict to secure a sense of belonging. The struggle between selfishness and caring, first encountered in our families, is played out in less familiar or predictable relationships. Choices, values, and consequences are clarified. Is having my way more important than friendship? What can I do when my friend doesn't care about what I want? Can we be happy together? Friendships will make us think and invite us to care; they lead us to forgiveness when we have strayed into selfishness.

Giving in friendship becomes a passageway from *me* to *we*. Giving is an act of leadership, where the giver proclaims, "You are important to me, and I care. I am willing to set aside for a time my own desires and give you my hands, heart, and spirit to fulfill what is important to you." Giving invites and encourages the other to enrich and deepen the loving experience by giving as well. A beautiful and potentially endless cycle of giving is set into motion. The experience of giving and receiving in friendship is emotionally exquisite and uplifting. It can generate an enduring peace and comfort, lasting for days or even a lifetime. Giving momentarily takes us outside of ourselves and frees us from the prison of aloneness and the shallowness and curse of selfishness. Giving forms a connection between people, which expands and is strengthened with every cycle of mutual giving and receiving.

The greatest leader of friendship the world has ever known was Jesus Christ, who gave completely of Himself in His teaching, miracles, love, life, death, and resurrection. He invites us into a profound friendship, promising us rewards beyond our wildest dreams, in this life and the next, if we will give our love and life in friendship with Him. He is available as our constant companion and confidant. We may talk with Him whenever we want and need. He understands us and how we feel better than anyone could. He is always thinking about our good, ready to comfort, guide, and help. With the foundation of His great friendship of all friendships, we are truly equipped to fulfill the divine promises of friendship with others. He asks us to follow His lead.

Only with the strength of a friendship with Jesus will we be strong enough to weather the storms of conflict and rejection that are surely to come in our friendships with others. With Him, our worth and value is secure and cannot be questioned. With Him, we have calm in the midst of turmoil. With Him, we have confidence that loving is the answer to all questions that really matter and that loving is the passageway for fulfilling desires, solving problems, and resolving conflicts. By working together, playing together, learning together, and worshiping together, people and friendships grow endlessly in the love of Jesus. Insisting upon friendship as the basis for relating with others is both an extraordinary gift and a protective shield for the slings and arrows of those who insist upon living selfishly.

No one could have too many friends. There will always be room for more in our lives. Everyone we meet is a potential friend, no matter how brief our experience with her and no matter what has happened in the past. The friendships of our youth prepare us for the most special friendship of our lifetime, the relationship between husband and wife. How important it truly is to abandon the idea of looking for an intimate mate and instead to seek and develop friendships. From the ranks of friendship, God will bring mates together in His foresight and love. More on this in a moment.

The norms, values, and practices of friendship apply in all human relationships: strangers, acquaintances, classmates and coworkers, relatives and enemies, the powerful and meek, rich and poor, sinner and saint—you name it. The fabric of our friendships has everything to do with the quality and joy of life, our meaning and purpose, our health and happiness, and our success and freedom. When you consider the place of friendship in our lives, you may wonder why is it not the most important subject taught from kindergarten through high school. Why not have college and graduate degrees in friendship? Why not dedicate the power of information, communications, and entertainment technologies to developing a culture of friendship? And why not align our economic, commercial, justice, and political systems in a spirit and practice of friendship?

Marriage

In the grand scheme of things, childhood and youth prepare us, program us, cultivate our perceptions and beliefs, and grow us into unique individuals with endless limitations, a few talents, assorted hurts, fears, and insecurities, a more or less flawed understanding of how the world works, and a drive for loving that rivals our instincts for survival. When we reach physical maturity, the deck is stacked for us to do something very foolish and actually quite selfish. We will look for someone to make us happy, to comfort and pleasure us, to like us and believe in us, "to be there" for us, to play with us, live for us, heal us, complete us, be our soul mate, be our orgasm partner, be ours, all in the name of love. Usually, we look for the mate without first establishing a true friendship. What a rude awakening it can be, some time later, after the idealized romantic high has faded, after lovemaking has become having sex, and after the reality of day-to-day life and making ends meet reveals that neither of you were whom you appeared and that both of you are unable to do what you hoped the other would do for you.

If you can accept that each of us, a momentary living speck in an infinite universe of time and space, is a deliberate and glorious creation with a purpose for eternal loving and not one more accident in a stream of countless accidents over twenty billion years, then wouldn't you defer to the Creator of it all to choose a perfect mate for you? And wouldn't you want to practice His idea of loving, as opposed to borrowing from the ideas of other people like you or inventing it on your own? The deep, full, and intimate love of our life without God is hopelessly complicated and impossible. With Him, it is simple. He asks us to love Him first with all our hearts, minds, souls, and strength, and to love others as ourselves, and He will take care of the rest.

Imagine, instead of looking for a mate, looking for God. Know anyone more attractive or important than the loving Creator of the universe? The real shocker is that God has been looking for you, hoping to get your attention, and wanting to love you perfectly and completely. Everything you have hoped to find in the most wonderful loving and intimate relationship, He offers—and so much more. The more you love Him, the more of His love you can absorb into your being, growing you more fully into the person He created you to be, a light for the love of Him and others.

Believe it or not, while you are busy loving God and others, He will choose and bring a truly loving mate into your life, and this person will first enter as a friend. Believing, trusting, and loving God provides a solid core or foundation for building true friendship. There will be no need to find someone else to complete you or make you happy. There will be no rush to intimacy. Carnal desires will be overshadowed by the simple joys and pleasures of friendship. In fact, helping each other to set aside sexual impulses until God has blessed the union of oneness with Him in marriage potently expands and deepens the friendship.

In the safety of friendship, men and women are free to really get to know one another. Since the faithful will allow God to choose their perfect mate, all but one relationship between men and women will remain friendships. Living with the focus of loving God and others will make obvious who our friends are and who our mate is. Our loving relationship with God, being our first and most important relationship, will by God's design require both man and woman to be spiritually bound in loving with Him. Friendships between men and women may begin with one or both being faithless. If God is truly blessing the relationship, both will have a loving relationship with God at the center of their lives before they commit to each other in marriage.

Whether we would like to admit it or not, there is no way to overcome our selfishness, our foolish pursuits of happiness in the world, or the exquisite and pervasive deception of conditional acceptance and rejection, without God. Relationships whose members are not lovingly connected with God are critically vulnerable to conflict, disappointment, detachment, betrayal, hurt, rejection, stagnation, demoralizing loss, addictions, and emptiness. If you are in a marriage with a mate who does not love God, all is not lost. Simply dedicate yourself to loving God with all your heart, mind, soul, and strength, and love your mate as yourself. Let God do the rest. One of two things will happen. In time, with God's love and yours, your mate will be saved and join you in a loving oneness with God. Or, your mate will become unfaithful, which is an indication that he or she has chosen to live without God and without true love in a foolish pursuit of happiness through selfishness. You will then be free by God's grace to leave the marriage, and as you go on loving God and others, trust that He will answer all your desires for loving.

In marriages filled with God's love, there is an abundance of the fruit of the Spirit: love, joy, peace, long-suffering, kindness, goodness, faithfulness, gentleness, and self-control (Galatians 5:22–23a). Husbands love their wives as Jesus loves all who believe in Him: humbly serving, leading faithfully, giving His all, and even giving His life for the good of His beloved. Wives are the helpmates of their husbands, collaborators for the fulfillment of loving God, each other, their children, and their families, friends, community, and worldly brothers and sisters. Husbands and wives extend to each other the unconditional acceptance that God has given to each of them. In mutual respect and committed peace, they share their desires and emotions with each other, pooling their talents, experience, energy, and passion to help each other and serve. Together, they make decisions, solve problems, and resolve conflicts, seeking the great wisdom and will of God. They face the challenges and losses of life together with God, growing ever more deeply in spirit and in love. They celebrate the great blessings of God together: His creation of their lives, bodies, minds, hearts, spirits, and souls; His great gifts of grace, mercy, forgiveness, redemption, love, and the beautiful and wondrous union of their being in sexual intimacy; and the miraculous collaboration with God that may begin a new life.

With lives rooted in God's love, friendship, and a blessed marital covenant for life, the way is prepared for children, the most important and challenging collaboration of loving that a husband and wife will undertake in their lifetimes. Just as they had formed a trinity with God in marriage, a mother and father form a trinity with each child. Loving between husband and wife is elaborated and matured through serving, leading, and loving their children together. For husbands and wives who may not be called to have children of their own, their love will likewise grow through active lives of service and the loving of others together.

Marriage is also a collaborative stewardship of the blessings and gifts of God's provision, which include children, time, talents, energy, financial resources, and love. Husbands and wives love God and each other when they gratefully receive these treasures, and consider together what God would like them to do with these blessings. It surely is tempting to consider these gifts as our own, to do with as we like; however, we must keep in mind how exceedingly brief this lifetime is compared to eternity; to whom all of these gifts truly belong; and His purpose for giving, which is furthering the kingdom of love.

As time passes and children grow into lives of their own, marriages enter a final stage of preparation for an eternity of loving. One by one, everything we ever thought was important, and everything that is important, will be lost, excepting one thing. We will lose our appearances, our strength, and the powers of our minds, health, material comforts, friends, and even our loved ones. In the end, we will be alone with God. We can love God and each other through these losses, becoming ever more clear about what is important and what is not, growing into the absolute fullness of loving, which will be the last thing we will lose in this life, a mere prelude of the glorious loving to come.

Parenting

The loving relationship of parent and child contains endless metaphors and references for all the relationships of our lifetimes. Certainly, the relationships of our lives, leading up to the moment we begin parenting, will profoundly affect the parents we will be. Only our relationships with God could be fuller spiritually than our relationships with our children. The parallel between our relationships with God and our relationships with our children is both direct and symbolic. God is our Father; we are His children. He gave us life; man and woman collaborate with God to conceive a new life. God demonstrates in His relationship with His son, Jesus, parenting perfection. Each of us can experience directly the unconditionally loving parenting of God, if we are open to it. Nothing could better prepare us for parenting than living fully in a loving relationship with God, as our brother Jesus demonstrated in His life.

Consider parenting from a spiritual perspective, and incredible wisdom follows. Love our children and others as our own children, just as our Father God loves us. Consider everyone a brother or sister in our eternal family with God. Give reverence and honor to our fathers and mothers, inspired by our reverence for God. Sadly, for a great many people, rejection has dimmed the light of love in these important family relationships and turned them into empty, hurtful objects to avoid. By His forgiveness and mercy, our Father shows us how to heal these wounds and redeem these relationships. Forgiving our mothers and fathers for how they may have hurt us and seeking their forgiveness for how we hurt them are important spiritual and emotional resolutions to prepare ourselves for parenting. As parents, we would be wise to give our children generous amounts of forgiveness and mercy, so that in time, they too will extend it to us, and others.

We have one Father, one spiritual parent. Just as it is His intention that husband and wife would form a loving oneness with Him for a joyous marriage, it is His desire that mother and father would form a loving oneness with Him as parents for the love of the children they have with Him. In a very real and practical way, a mother and father collaborate with God and each other in the parenting of children. He has provided a model, the parenting manual (the Bible, particularly the book of Proverbs), and moment-to-moment counseling by His indwelling Spirit. He has created in us a capacity, heart, and purpose for parenting and given us a rich life experience of parenting from the point of view of our childhood, whether we consider it a good one or a bad one. He brings each of us together with a mate to creatively consider and use these gifts for the nurturing and guiding of children. He wants a mother and father to complement one another and parent together as one; two parents are greater than the sum of their two parts.

Just as God carefully planned and prepared for the conception and birth of His son Jesus with a perfect and seamless understanding of the past and future, it is vital for a mother and father to seek and trust the will of God on the matter of when to have children. On our own we are capable of amazing foolishness, such as having children when we haven't grown up; when we didn't intend to have them; when we simply wanted someone to love or to love us; because it is the next step in the progression of life; to save a marriage; because they are affordable; or for fun and amusement. How easy it is to pass along to children the sins of their parents and lay down obstacles for the children to grow in love! Ideally, mother and father will love God with all their hearts, minds, souls, and strength, and love each other as themselves; also, ideally both will have a calling from God to be a parent that is joyously and responsibly received.

To conceive a child in the context of God's love and timing is one of the greatest blessings of life, and it is one that can beneficially affect generations to come. Immediately, the bond between husband and wife deepens and expands simultaneously with a growing bond for the developing life in the mother's womb. The man and woman will be challenged to set aside whatever selfishness remains for the cause of love. The collaboration of husband and wife spiritually, emotionally, and practically during the term of the pregnancy is the passageway to becoming a family. The emphasis on marital intimacy gently gives way to the generative intimacy of parenting, which ultimately adds great character and maturity to the marriage. As husband and wife become father and mother, they combine their loving powers of giving, forming a new trinity with the child. As father and mother help each other prepare for the birth and then go through the momentous birthing experience together, husband and wife enter a new realm of loving. After all, they have done something miraculous together, something more important than anything they will ever do, something purifying that reveals what really is important.

At birth, the seed of loving planted by God in our DNA begins to grow and bloom in glorious beauty. The newborn is to his parents as each of us is to God: vulnerable, helpless, and completely dependent for life. Present, attentive, fiercely protective (rejecting rejection), tender, attuned, and selflessly willing to care and address whatever is needed, God and parents pursue connections and bonds for the sake of survival, security, loving, and guidance. God and parents serve and are responsive to the needs expressed, providing comfort and peace, which grows and deepens the bond between parents and their newborn and between God and His children. Just as parents can experience joy each time their infant is contented, so God is likely blessed when we trust in His provision. The potential for lifelong and eternal mutually enriching loving is foreshadowed on the day of our birth.

With every need that is met and every day that passes, the bond grows more elaborate and stronger. At first, the infant cannot do anything deliberately to address a need of her parents, just as there is nothing we can do to address a need of God. What genetically and developmentally unfolds is a hardwired capacity to express needs and respond with comfort when needs are met. By the grace and design of God, newborns reward their parents' giving in a profoundly meaningful and heartfelt way. In the same way, God has gifted each of us with an innate ability to search for and respond to His love.

All the elements of collaboration are purely apparent at birth. Indeed, the collaboration that brought about conception seamlessly continued between embryo and mother through the term of pregnancy, only to take on a different form once the umbilical cord was cut. The infant reflexively expresses need; in acceptance, respect, and peace, the parents acknowledge the need and together with the infant, look for a way to address it. In the end, both the infant and the parents' needs are fulfilled. By their actions, parents give the infant the experience of loving—leading, modeling, and teaching the most important lesson she will ever learn. The infant guides her parents to understand her needs and to learn how best to address them, teaching the parents anew the importance of selfless giving and loving that was perfectly exemplified in Jesus' life.

The bonds of love with our children and with God can be elaborated endlessly, since every moment brings an opportunity for a loving collaboration. With maturity and experience children acquire the skills to collaborate creatively with others to obtain their desires and goals; to explore the world and their capacities; to experiment and learn; to solve problems; to understand and manage emotions, both their own and others'; to resolve conflicts, both within themselves and with others; and, all along the way, to expand their loving with others and God.

On the dark side, the newborn confronts his parents and the world with an unabashedly selfish nature. When parents gaze upon their newborn, they are looking in a mirror. The infant is a captive of egocentrism. The infant's limitations are endless, just like everyone else's, although more obviously. With maturity, children gain the ability to notice others; to appreciate others' feelings and desires; to understand cause and effect, how their actions affect others; and to realize the awesome power and responsibility of free will. Loving parents will nurture and guide their children to develop these abilities and this power for loving purposes, first and foremost by their own example.

Like us, children are naturally oriented to get what they want as quickly and easily as possible. Like the back to the womb fantasy, we have within us a yearning for every momentary desire to be effortlessly and automatically fulfilled. The modern world caters to this disposition, and Satan exploits it to prevent and undermine loving. Children prefer parents and others to adapt to them, to give to them with less of an interest to give in return, since it can be a messy distraction from the business of pursuing their desires. This tendency resonates deeply in all our spirits. In essence, it is our sin nature. Just as we need a loving God to correct us and guide us away from this nature toward loving, our children need loving parents who can do the same. These parents will lead the way proactively by modeling collaboration in all their dealings with the children, with each other, and with other people. Just as God can use bad for good, each time our children act selfishly, when the opportunity for collaboration is present, parents can orchestrate a corrective experience involving forgiveness, the practice of collaborative skills, and the making of reparations with whoever was involved. This loving form of discipline, applied consistently with acceptance, respect, and peace, gives children a "no lose" choice: they can live in loving collaboration with others or live to obtain what they desire. To choose collaboration, they will first need to redeem themselves by repairing what their selfishness disturbed and then restore a loving bond by collaborating to meet everyone's desires. Just as God will not bless us for sin, loving parents will not fulfill their children's desires outside of loving collaboration. In time, children will learn the only way to get what they want is through loving. Along the way, whatever selfish habits children may have will be weakened, since they simply won't work. Just as God continues to accept us unconditionally, even when we are in sin, parents can offer loving collaboration as a way of life for their children, while refusing any participation in the adversarial and selfish pursuit of desires.

Just as God nurtures and guides His children, nurturing and guiding are the two vital aspects of parental love—these aspects are revealed by what we do and how we do it. Nurturing establishes safety and security in a physical, personal, and spiritual sense, encouraging children to explore and experiment peacefully in the world. Guidance passes on to children what the parents have learned that the children may use in their own lives, often sparing them dangers and hardships. When parents nurture well, they are providing the highest order of guidance for living in a loving way. When parents guide with love, the wisdom passed along will be welcomed and treasured by children and will be profoundly nurturing.

In adolescence, the nervous system approaches maturity, so that youth obtain all the capacities of adult logical thought. Of course, with these newfound powers comes a drive to use them and a growing reluctance to take direction from parents, who understand all too well that their adolescents have little experience using the powers of their minds. The neurological maturity of adolescence ushers in a new era of relationship between parents and their teenagers. Parents who practice acceptance, respect, rejection of rejection, peacemaking, active listening, specific expression of desire, and collaboration can seamlessly transition from childhood to adolescence. This form of loving guidance allows the adolescent to use the powers of thinking to gain experience in a safe, supportive context that encourages what is good, true, responsible, and caring, while blocking what is harmful, hurtful, or sinful. Instead of lecturing or giving advice, parents pose thought-provoking questions to give their teenagers practice using the powers of thinking and to encourage them to consider the values that will direct their free will. Just like God the Father, parents will bless and support choices that are truly good for the teen and others (obedient to the will of God) and withhold support for choices that are harmful or sinful, within the bounds of safety, allowing natural consequences to run their course. To encourage an adultlike responsibility and accountability, loving parents will give their teens direct advice only when it is asked for, just as God reveals His will, either when we seek it or when we experience the consequences of not seeking it. Parents who are living a loving relationship with God and their teenagers are modeling, mentoring, and discipling the best way life could be lived, without forcing compliance and inviting rebellion. The stark choices and associated consequences of living in a loving way are contrasted with living in a selfish way, as a final stage of preparation for the teenager before entering into adulthood. Parents take their lead from their graceful, merciful, forgiving, loving, righteous, and uncompromising God.

When young people have concluded their education and preparation for their adult lives and literally or figuratively leave home, the parent-child relationship becomes a uniquely loving relationship between adults. In no other adult relationship, except in marriage, could there be this history, breadth, and depth of loving. The adult parental relationship is a bridge to loving God and others. For young adults who were blessed with God-loving parents, they move on, in faith, hope, and love, elaborating and enriching the relationship with their mothers and fathers endlessly in their passages through life. Sadness and loss may visit parents and young adults who do not know the fullness of loving God and each other when the young people leave home. These emotions call attention to what is missing and can inspire young adults and parents to seek fulfillment or propel them into greater darkness. Storms of blame and rejection will divide and must be resisted with forgiveness. Because God loves all of us, there is always hope for prodigal children and prodigal parents to find their ways to love.

As time brings young adults into maturity and parents become grandparents, loving can exponentially prosper and bloom. Through the loving pathways of friendship and marriage, the cycle of life comes full circle, linking past and future together. Sharing a loving life, mature adults and parents develop bonds with spouses, their families, and their friends, all a part of a loving community to welcome and support the next generation and each other. The birth of grandchildren forms yet another trinity of loving, reflecting the glory of God. Grandparents, parents, and child, each with a unique perspective of loving each other, form a loving oneness that foreshadows eternity. This crown of loving endures and shines brilliantly as aging surrenders everything that for a season seemed important. In the end, love is all there is. The love of God and others is the passageway through death to eternal life, established by Jesus Christ, the Master of love. The grandparents leave the parents and grandchildren with a priceless and timeless loving inheritance.

Church

Because we are children of God, created for a loving destiny, it follows that we would gather together as a family to worship the God who loves us. We love God through a personal, intimate relationship in daily life with Him and through a public sharing and celebration of love for Him. The two go together and are mutually encouraging. Our personal faith and love for God can be a comfort for others, and even inspire them. The Bible tells us that God routinely uses and directs those who love Him to draw others into His great circle of love. Where two or more are gathered together for Him, He will be there in His magnificent Spirit, serving and blessing. Our brothers and sisters in God may share their joy, love, and help with us if we have lost our ways or have trials. Church is so much more than a place to meet with God. It is a family that comes together to love God and each other.

A church that is filled with the love of God is a family of families, where everyone is a brother or sister. Acceptance, respect, peace, understanding, help, and caring bind each one to all others as cells are bound together in the human body, each depending on the others for life and for the health of the whole. The love of friendships, husbands and wives, and parents and children springs forth from the love of God, becoming a mighty river of love that protects, nourishes, fortifies, comforts, heals, provides, guides, bears, endures, and radiates hope. We all belong in a church family, pouring the full measure of our love into the mighty river, drinking our fill, and cleansing our bodies, minds, and spirits with its living waters.

God has told us how to do this with passion and eloquence in the Bible, His Word, which is the most profound assurance of His endless love for us. It is tragic but not surprising that ignorance, misunderstandings, distortions, confusion, and lies abound concerning this most sacred and important book. God has many determined and powerful enemies, consumed with ambition and pride, who have nothing but contempt for Him and for love. The Bible is God's own voice, telling us the story of where we came from, why we're here, the purpose and meaning of life, the truth, the way to live, what lies beyond time and space, who He is, and how He loves us. He tells us everything we need to know. He gives us the human operator's manual from the one and only Manufacturer. This is a living book that will protect its readers from the spirits of darkness with the sword of God and fill their beings with His own Spirit, revealing the wisdom of God in intimate and practical forms.

The Bible is the lifeblood of God's church. It is an invitation to a loving relationship with God. The more we realize the passion and urgency of His love and desire to speak to us personally, the more we will be humbled, awed, grateful, consumed with love for Him, and completely committed to give Him our lives. This is the heart of worship. This gives glory to God, who endlessly blesses His children with love. By worshiping God together, church families are empowered by the Spirit of God to share each other's joys and burdens, to study and apply God's Word in their lives, to raise up the young in the light of God's truth, to reach out to the lost, to serve the will of God, and to love each other.

Community

Beyond the thresholds of our homes lies the community. Neighbors and neighborhoods, schools and businesses, law enforcement and public safety, local governments, recreation and entertainment venues, social clubs and activities, medical and social services providers, and charities and voluntary organizations are all embedded in a broader social and cultural context determined by geography, economics, demography, communications, and communities of communities comprising political systems. Like people, communities come in all shapes, sizes, and characters. Some may be fragmented, impoverished, cold, or uncaring, while others may be inviting, capable, resourceful, and compassionate. Most communities are a mixture of these qualities. Communities can be as unique and different as people. They are the grand stages where people come together to make their way through life. They are repositories for the resources of knowledge, skill, creativity, energy, love, support, and power; where community members make deposits and withdrawals for addressing the needs and desires of its members. They are also the collective pools of its members' limitations, ignorance, hurt, and fear. Some individuals and families give more than they take, while others take more than they give. Some communities also may be giving, while others are self-serving, depending on the moral outlook of those in power and their ability to love.

Loving, especially faith-filled loving, is contagious and inspiring. To love a neighbor with respect, peace, and collaboration in day-to-day life is a gift that will likely be returned and shared with other neighbors. Giving is better than receiving, because it sets in motion a potentially endless exchange of giving, which joyfully enriches security and well-being. Some neighbors who may be hurt or lost, untrusting, and convinced isolation is necessary for safety may be cold or rejecting of loving. Still, loving is its own reward, will not return void, and can in time win over those who need it most.

The neighborhood is a microcosm of the world. Each family could be considered a country unto itself, with domestic and foreign policies, and each with its own customs and language. The differences can easily create barriers and conflict, and yet for those who are loving, there are opportunities for mutual understanding and growth. The cynical may say, why bother? But truly, who among us would choose darkness over light? Even a single small light in darkness can make seeing possible. An act of kindness is liberating for both the giver and receiver. One family, determined to live in a loving way, will sooner or later draw the neighborhood into the light.

At the tender age of five, children take a big step out into the community by going to school. Although from kindergarten through high school there may never be a single class devoted to loving, every day will offer many lessons about what loving is and is not. Each child will bring to school her own habits for getting what she wants, managing emotions, solving problems, and dealing with conflicts. Most children will come to school with love deficits and insecurities spawned by rejection. Every child will observe and learn unconsciously from how the teachers treat them and other students and how students treat each other, the teacher, and them. It is for the most part an unscripted curriculum, despite efforts on the part of the schools to develop norms and rules. The subtle communication of eye movements, facial gestures, tones of voice, selective listening, and conditional acceptance and rejection are well established when children enter school.

Schools are communities unto themselves. Our children spend a significant part of their youth living and learning in these communities, which can powerfully shape who they will become. The dynamics of conditional acceptance and rejection draw our children to conform to the values of cliques, which for the most part are dominated by unhealthy youth with loving deficits. Great importance is given to fitting in, as opposed to standing out. Youths are constantly comparing themselves with others, measuring their worth and value on a yardstick of conditional acceptance and rejection. Insecurities and confusion grow in this social stew. Increasingly, youths become obsessed with themselves, how they look, how they act, and how they can establish themselves as people who will be noticed and accepted by others. They are yearning to be important and ultimately to be loved. However, they are lost without a map.

There likely has never been a time in our history when the value of loving has more urgently needed to be the supreme and overriding guideline for acting and relating in the communities of schools. It is a value that must be embraced and actively promoted by everyone involved in schooling, including the wider community, administration, faculty, staff, students, parents, and families. It is the value that can bring safety, security, and peace to schools, so that young people can explore, experiment, and learn about the world around them and about their own talents and possibilities.

Loving comprises the critical set of skills for living productively, successfully, meaningfully, and happily in the world. There is no knowledge more valuable than loving.

When young people mature into adults and complete their formal education, they will enter the community of work. Directly or indirectly, working involves taking care of the needs and desires of others to obtain the means to take care of ourselves and those we love. Our employers have work for us to do, a quality standard for performance, and a timeframe for the work to be completed. When we fulfill an employer's desires or expectations, the employer will provide compensation and benefits. The employer is both a customer of other employers and a server of customers, engaged in various collaborations of giving and receiving.

Both employers and employees are inclined to give greater importance to what they want, as opposed to what the other may want or what customers may want. Often there are material rewards for those who are "ambitious" or "assertive," determined to find a way of getting back more than they may give. This manner of working sets into motion a stream of consequences, many of which can be both unappreciated and harmful. Souls are lost on material enrichment. Relationships are drained of love and meaning. Stress and conflict are unleashed. People hurt one another, becoming increasingly isolated, needy, or greedy, and turn to addictions for comfort. Resources are spent and not replenished. The natural and social environments are degraded and polluted. Ultimately, such employees bite the hand that feeds them, and such employers kill the goose that lays the golden eggs.

Loving belongs in the community of work, just as it belongs in all the relationships of our lives. Loving happens to be good for business. What we do for work is not as important as how we do it. Loving employers collaborate with customers and employees, treating both the way they would like to be treated.

Likewise, loving employees relate with the employer and other employees collaboratively, treating all the way they would like to be treated. Working this way leads to job satisfaction and security for the employee, and it leads to productivity, wise stewardship of resources, and customer loyalty for the employer. Streams of positive consequences flow out in all directions. Workers and their families are healthier and happier. Employers grow their businesses on solid foundations, encourage customers and other businesses to adopt the loving ethic, and give a vital gift to the community that will be returned many times over.

Living by the ethics of love inspires people to serve others. The needs, locally and globally, are vast, in large part because a critical mass of people and nations behave in unloving ways, without the foundation of loving with God. It is curious how serving and helping others produces a measure of joy and hope in both the giver and receiver. Many speculate or believe this phenomenon can be explained by principles of psychology and sociology. Attachment and bonding dynamics are being exercised or social approval for good deeds enhances "self-esteem." These and other explanations, however, just don't seem to go far or deep enough. Jesus gave us the answer to this riddle. It is better to give than to receive.

Our nature orients us to live by the dictum that it is better to receive than to give. We are easily fooled into believing that having what we want will make us happy. This way of living is a retreat from hurt and a cynical conviction there is no such thing as love. Looking out for number one and taking care of yourself becomes more important than other people. But this way of life is the problem, not the solution, and it is doomed. It weakens or destroys connections with others, cutting off its practitioners from the means to manage their needs and from love, leaving them imprisoned by their appetites, alone, and without hope. This way of life spreads hurt and rejection in the world like a virus.

It is truly better to give than to receive. Living by this motto sets in motion endless exchanges of giving. Doing good and committing random acts of kindness in our neighborhoods and communities benefits our health, spirits, souls, others, and the quality of community life. Spending time as a volunteer will touch the hearts of others, as well as your own.

Counseling

One shining example of God's great wisdom and sense of humor is that He created each one of us with endless limitations. What we do not know and what we cannot do is infinite. We are absolutely hopeless if we try to make our ways through the world on our own. Whenever we find ourselves at the limit of our experience, there is an opportunity for us to share in a loving experience, which we could call help. To reach out to God or another person with a request for help is a loving act that can bless everyone involved. All of us depend on each other for much more help than we likely realize. The food we eat, the clothing we wear, the home we live in, the car we drive and the road we drive it on, the power and communications that come into our homes, the schools our children attend, the doctors we visit for health care, our places of work, where we shop, the communities we live in, and our states and nations all depend upon countless numbers of people helping each other to function. We are completely and elegantly interdependent on each other for help.

It is not accidental that many people believe that using help is a sign of weakness, ignorance, or shame. Our conditionally accepting and rejecting world isolates us from one another and invites comparisons with one another, causing endless anxieties about our value, capability, and lovability. In this context, many regard self-reliance, self-sufficiency, and independence as virtues of strength and respect. To be sure, there is a balance to strike between using well the talents and resources we have and seeking the help of others when we are at our limits. However, our experiences of rejection create yet another illusion that what is good is bad—namely, seeking help. We were never meant to live alone; rather, we were meant to live for love. The giving and receiving of help are forms of loving.

On the day of each of our births, it is obvious to all that we are virtually helpless, dependent on mothers and fathers and others for our very survival and care. While the form of our helplessness and dependency certainly changes as we mature through the journeys of our lives, we are, in the grand scheme of things, just as helpless and dependent every day of our lives. No wonder God encourages us to be completely dependent on Him, seeking His advice and counsel on matters great and small. Since God is the giver of life, He will often use people in our lives to give us the help we need. Children are given parents, who are given children, each helping the other to grow and mature. Friends help each other in facing challenges and sharing joy in the passages of life. Husbands and wives grow each other in the expansive realm of loving.

Helping involves doing for another what he may not be able to do for himself, or by himself. The help may come in the form of information or knowledge, a skill, nurturing and encouragement, or the power to achieve a desire or accomplish something. Help may be practical, such as giving a friend a ride to the store, money for a charity, or helping someone hang a window. Help may come in the form of service, such as the post office, a bank, a dentist, an attorney, a carpenter, or a breeder of horses. We may find help in the Yellow Pages, over a cup of coffee with an acquaintance, in a story about the life of someone we never met, in a Bible verse, or in the intimate fellowship of a counseling relationship.

From the base of our infinite ignorance, we are all in need of counseling for the vital matters of living: developing the health of our bodies, the talents and potential of our minds, the power of loving, stewardship of local and global environments, and most importantly, a mature spiritual relationship with God. Unfortunately, just as the practice of love has been misunderstood, misused, and perverted, so too has the practice of counseling. Most forms of counseling have become self-serving. The helper is helping herself more than the helped. There are far too many counselors who are helping to inflate their sense of their own importance, power, feeling of well-being, or bank account more than they are truly helping others. It can be bewildering for help-seekers to find trustworthy counselors in the matrix of "Allied Health Professionals," managed-care insurance companies, and pastoral ministries. They have created a language and culture unto themselves.

For perspective, we must never forget we are fearfully and wonderfully made. The human body, mind, and soul form a trinity in one, which speaks to us about being made in His image and about His glory and love. Our being is for relationship with Him and others. We must, therefore, give reverence to His design for the workings of the mind.

Science, above all, is a tool of observation. Its objective is to reveal truth in the nature of relationships, whether that be biology, chemistry, physics, mathematics, psychology, or human relationships. Science is observing God's creation. The mind was the organ God chose for belief, for love, and for science to reveal His glory and majesty.

Knowing this, the enemy of God has chosen the mind as a critical point of attack. With his deception and lethal infection of rejection, the enemy has wreaked havoc with the beliefs of man and human history. Science has been perverted as well, since only

God is capable of absolute objectivity and truth. Nevertheless, science is not without merit, and not all the mind is defiled.

Man has developed a science for helping people, which in no way diminishes God, even when practiced by people who are ungodly. God is in loving, even when the actor of love is not in God. Of course, the social sciences, like any science, are not infallible. These sciences fall short of truth and generate considerable rubbish and narcissism, as does any endeavor of man. But we should restrain ourselves from throwing the baby out with the bathwater. God did not make us absolutely incapable of doing anything right or make us helplessly depend on Him to do everything good for us. On the contrary, with the gift of free will, He made us collaborators with Him for good and for love. Helping us is one of the ways He loves us, and seeking His help is one of the ways we love Him, just as helping each other is an act of love for Him.

In my nearly forty-year career I have counseled with and without God. I find counseling with God immeasurably better, more helpful, and more enjoyable. Earlier, as I was drawn to understand the essence of helping others, of comforting pain and grief, and of solving difficult problems with the people trusting in my care, I was, without knowing it, taught by them and led by God to understand the truth of loving. Now, a Christian who happens to be a psychologist, I counsel people who love God and who do not know Him. I do all my counseling with God. He has illuminated brilliantly what truth I could find before I knew Him. Every day I pray He will use me to reveal His love, especially to those who don't know Him. It is my mission.

Since a counseling relationship is another form of a loving relationship based upon mutual acceptance, respect, rejection of rejection, peace, listening, and collaboration, and since, directly or indirectly, the focus of counseling will involve the vital matters of living, I believe it is crucial that the process of counseling be present with God; that the counselor is living a loving relationship with God and others; that the life and teachings of Jesus, the ultimate Counselor, inspire and guide all that is done through the perfect help of the Holy Spirit; and that the love of God and Jesus be the healing force and the foundation for living a loving life.

God

I have saved the best for last. The last shall be first. In the Great Commandment, Jesus taught us to love God with all our hearts, minds, souls, and strength first. Love God, our Creator, Savior, and wonderful Counselor, with everything we have, every moment. Recognizing we are alive, there is nothing more important that we could do, wherever we happen to be, according to the God who made us, than to love Him. In the beginning, however, it is quite a conundrum to live this way.

First of all, it's difficult to do two things at once, such as living in this real world and loving God at the same time. There are a multitude of moments where it is difficult to figure out how you could love God—for example, standing in line at the grocery store, reading a newspaper, mowing the lawn, caring for a loved one in pain, ruminating over how bills will be paid, dealing with someone who ripped you off, or rolling over in your car in the grip of terror. The more one contemplates this question, the more clear it becomes that God can be with us wherever we go, any time, no matter what we're doing, and He can be the most incredible friend, mate, parent, and counselor we could ever dream of having. Wanting God to be with you, and being open to how you may act at any given moment to love Him, are two beautiful ways of loving Him.

Besides being always available, God accepts us unconditionally, even with our limitations, faults, and sins. He yearns to forgive, and He will never reject us, even though we may ignore Him, wander off on our own, squander what He has given to us, and reject Him. The only thing He will not forgive is if we deliberately reject His Spirit, whose purpose is to help us develop a loving relationship with His Son Jesus, who offers us the only way to be with God. To treasure that acceptance—Grace—and to receive it thankfully and joyfully are important ways of loving God. We all search endlessly in the world for acceptance from others. For the most part, it is a frustrating labor and often disappointing, if not hurtful. Even our most dear loved ones are capable of rejection at times of weakness, stress, or conflict. God offers a perfect acceptance by way of His grace. We need not work to obtain it. We love Him simply by our seeking and accepting it.

Being God's children, He respects and reveres us more than any person ever could. He offers us a safety and peace that is beyond understanding. He is always listening and understanding us better than we can understand ourselves. What He wants from us is simple, clear, and profoundly good for us—namely, to love Him and others. He is the most capable collaborator we will ever know. He will not force us to do anything or to make any choice. He wants to be intimately involved in our lives and is delighted more than we will ever know when we choose to be with Him. If we invite Him, He will live in us. He will defend and protect us in the great spiritual war. With Him, the rejections that others give to us can no longer hurt; in fact, with His peace and love, we will have compassion for these lost souls. The rejections of the past will be healed. Together with Him, all problems can be solved, all emotions can be comforted, and all conflicts can be resolved.

With Him, the desires of our hearts can be obtained, provided only that fulfilling the desires truly would be good for us and that He doesn't have something much better in mind. With Him, we are capable of loving others with profound depth, far beyond any loving without Him. Considering all of this, why wouldn't we want God to be with us always? Could there be any one more deserving of our love?

Loving God begins with welcoming Him into our lives and accepting Him unconditionally. Having a relationship with God, who is not present in a literal, physical sense, is a paradox in view of our relationships with family, friends, and others who may be with us. But, just as our relationships with others do not cease when we are separate, our relationship with God may be continuous even though He cannot be physically experienced. When we accept God unconditionally and dedicate our human capacity to believe completely, while rejecting belief in the myriad false gods, such as the idols of our world, and rejecting the foolish belief in ourselves apart from God, it is as if we have passed through the gates of heaven. He becomes our constant companion. We begin a conversation, or prayer, that will never end with the one true God, whom we can trust absolutely and respect with unrestrained reverence. This is a relationship unlike any other. God's love for us is an inspiration for us to love Him in the very best way we can from moment to moment, an uplifting way of living that grows our power and creativity for loving Him and others as time goes by.

Listening to God, learning about Him, and seeking His will, or what He wants from us, is one of the most important ways we can love Him and resolve the conundrum of how to love Him with all our heart, mind, soul, and strength. He speaks to us through His Word, the Holy Bible. This is a book unlike any other. Consider it the greatest story ever told, only it is all true; the perfectly complete portrait of reality; the answer to human beings' search for meaning; the human operator's manual; and an endlessly profound discourse on the nature of love. It is timelessly relevant, immediately accessible, and a living, breathing message from God about everything and anything we shall encounter in our lives. Through this book, God speaks to each of us intimately, simply, and purely, revealing who we truly are by way of who He is. This one book contains more wisdom than all the books ever written. In His Word, God shines His light of truth into the darkness of the world and the human soul. Passionately, He shows us how we can love Him and others in all possible situations.

The more we read and study the Word of God, the more His Spirit inspires and moves in our lives. It is the purpose and intention of His Spirit to guide our every choice and act, as if we were Jesus, the Son of God. The Spirit moves in an endless variety of unique and personal ways. Sometimes we simply have an immediate revelation upon reading a verse or passage of Scripture. Sometimes, mysteriously, He will guide us to a particular verse. Sometimes He may speak to us in our own thoughts or through intuition, providing an answer or advice on matters we have talked with God about in prayer. Sometimes He guides us by way of our emotions, affirming we are on the right track when we are at peace and calling us to be vigilant, careful, and especially loving when our emotions are uncomfortable. Sometimes, He may move someone we know to take action or to bring us a message in loving fellowship, or perhaps the Spirit will use a perfect stranger. The more we seek God by meditating on His Word, the more His Spirit will reveal and move in our lives, and the more our capacity for loving God and others will grow. The believing, seeking, following, serving, praising, thanking, and worshiping God gradually becomes a way of life as His Spirit transforms us from whom the world, and we, made ourselves to be, to whom *He* made us to be. Loving Him is the passageway for our own transformation, liberation, and joy. With the giving and receiving of godly love at the core of our being, our love of friends, mates, children, church family, and community flourishes and reveals His glory.

The End as Beginning

> Then God said,"Let the earth bring forth grass,
> the herb that yields seed, and the fruit tree that
> yields fruit according to its kind, whose seed is in
> itself on the earth"; and it was so.
>
> —Genesis 1:11 (NKJV)

In soil one hundred times more acidic than the average garden, God planted the first seeds of wild blueberries. Underground stems, called rhizomes, rooted the plants as they grew into a community or "clone," spreading out up to two hundred and fifty feet squared, seventy percent of the plant remaining underground. The sturdy, adaptable, ground-hugging bushes endure the bitter cold and wind of winter and the blistering heat of summer sun. In the spring, tiny bell-shaped flowers with a soft white and pink hue offer sweet nectar to the bees of the field that carry the berries' pollen from plant to plant. The union within each bell of fitting genes follows God's design to form a small, delicious, deep blue fruit. Atop each wild blueberry is the base of its earlier flower, a calyx in the shape of a five-pointed star. Indian elders told the legend that during a time of starvation, the Great Spirit sent these "star berries" down from the night of heaven to relieve the hunger of His children.

Modern research has uncovered many natural compounds in wild blueberries that are beneficial to our health, such as polymers to cleanse away harmful bacteria, manganese to maintain a healthy heart, and anthocyanin, the phytonutrient responsible for the berries' deep blue color, a powerful antioxidant that protects against oxidative cell damage that can lead to conditions like Alzheimer's disease, cancer, and heart disease, while softening the aging process, improving memory, and promoting good vision and urinary tract health.

Here is a fruit that protects us from harm and gives us long lives with strong vision, hearts, and minds. Here is an endlessly loving gift from God, revealing how important we all are to Him and how gracious and glorious He is. And in this simple, humble fruit there lies the substance and wisdom of the greatest spiritual food of all, love.

> "The sun shall no longer be your light by day, nor for brightness shall the moon give light to you; but the LORD will be to you an everlasting light, and your God your glory..." Isaiah 60:19 (NKJV)

ON THE path beyond the crossroads, you and the woman become one with the light, which is the essence of good, truth, peace, and love, radiating in all directions, timelessly. The sense of being loved and loving is pure, perfect, complete, vast, endless, and joyous. The barriers of their own bodies, minds, and spirits disappear. No longer are they separate. They know they are parts of one body, one mind, one heart, and one Spirit, as if it has always been so. Still, their own beings continue as well, shining beautifully in the brilliance of the light.

The light came into the world where there was darkness, touching the lives of the sick, hungry, thirsty, homeless, lost, broken, and alone: a little boy, sitting sadly on the steps of his empty home; a mother and wife, overwhelmed with responsibility, aching for the comfort of love; a woman tortured by rejection, who had given up all hope; a young mother who turned away from the darkness, searching for the light; a lost man who became broken trying to find himself; and countless others.

Being a part of the light, giving comfort, hope, and love, the woman and you are passionately alive and utterly selfless in devotion to serving the light and all the light can touch.

As the light beams brightly over the crossroads of each one's life and over the land and sea, it glows in the beautiful homes and gardens of the golden city and in the hearts of all who are touched; it even falls softly upon the fields of the lowly blueberry, fulfilling in just one of its boundless ways our magnificent Father's wonderful prophecy of love.

> ...that the world may know that Thou hast sent Me, and hast loved them, as Thou hast loved Me ... that the love wherewith Thou hast loved Me may be in them, and I in them. John 17:23, 26(KJV)

Appendix I
Loving

Highland

Thomas J. Gaffney, Psy.D.
Psychologist and Founder
E-mail: highlandsanctuary@fairpoint.net
www.mainechristiancare.com

*Loving is treating others the way I want to be treated
and asking and insisting others do the same.*

1. ***Accept without condition*** opinions, feelings, preferences, choices, and desires; ask/insist that others do the same for you, for their sake and yours.
2. ***Reject rejection.*** The selfish pursuit of desires that is manifested by conditionally accepting or rejecting others is unacceptable; ask/insist others pursue their desires in the loving way, for their sake and yours.
3. ***Respect.*** We are all children of God: priceless and unique living beings with bodies, minds and souls, no more or less important than anyone else. In word

and deed, let's treat each other with the reverence we deserve.

4. **Make peace.** We are each responsible for making and keeping peace and calm. If one of us is not doing this, let's stop, restore our own peace, help the other, and practice forgiveness.

5. **Actively listen.** Let's find out what is important to each other, what each of us wants to see happen in a specific and positive form.

6. **Express desires.** Let's help each other describe what we want specifically and positively, in the here and now.

7. **Collaborate.** Let's search *together* for ways to help each other fulfill our desires, and let's not rest until we are both content.

This is the way to learn, make decisions, and take care of our desires, feelings, problems, and conflict.

The first shall be last and the last shall be first.
It is better to give than to receive.
Let all that you do, be done in love.

Loving

... treating others the way you want to be treated,
and insisting others do the same.

Accept without Condition

Spiritual Acceptance

- Grace—the unmerited favor of God—the basis for our creation, forgiveness, salvation, justification, election, and spiritual gifts (Ephesians 1:7; Romans 3:24, 11:5–6; Ephesians 2:8–9; Romans 12:6).
- Faith—the complete and unconditional acceptance, trust, and love of God. Trust in the LORD with all your heart, and do not lean on your own understanding. In all your ways acknowledge Him, and He will make your paths straight. Proverbs 3:5–6(NASB)

Self-Acceptance

- God alone has given you importance by creating you and giving you life, a body, a mind, and a soul; by Jesus, the Son of God, giving His life to eternally save yours; by the Holy Spirit dwelling within you to guide and grow you into the image of Jesus. He has done all of this in order to have a loving relationship with you forever.

- There is nothing you or others can think, say, or do in your life that will raise or lower the importance God gave you. In the eyes of God, we are all equal.
- Treat yourself the way God treats you and the way you want others to treat you. Treasure and care for the life, body, mind, heart, and soul you have.

Acceptance in Relationships

- You have a responsibility to accept others unconditionally for who they are as children of God, for the utter uniqueness of their lives, and for the exercise of their free will.
- Accept, without tampering, others' opinions, thoughts, beliefs, feelings, preferences, desires, choices, hopes, and dreams. View these as others' most valued belongings.
- Ask others to accept you unconditionally when they are not, and insist upon it for their own good and for the sake of your relationship as a prerequisite for continuing your experience with them. Make a stand for loving as the most important act anyone can do at any moment.
- Be mindful of what you say and do, how you say and do it, and how others receive the message you are sending, and be ready to affirm acceptance.

Loving

Rejecting Rejection

Spiritual Rejection

- Lucifer, the most beautiful of all the angels and worship leader of heaven (Ezekiel 28:12–19), was the first to choose to turn away from loving God and His love; instead he decided to only value and believe in himself (which is sin). (See Isaiah 14:12–14.)
- Renamed Satan (the Adversary), he was cast out of heaven by God, along with a third of the angels loyal to him, to possess the earth.
- In the garden of Eden, Satan deceived Eve, whose nature and purpose was to love God and Adam, to only value herself for the first time.
- The fall from God's grace set the nature of human beings as creatures who would value themselves above loving God and others.

Self-Rejection

- As young children, we are only aware of our own experience and desires.
- We are powerfully motivated to satisfy our desires.
- We draw on our own experiences to satisfy our desires, often thinking ourselves to be the sources of all our methods.
- As we come into conflict with others' desires, we can come to believe we are unwanted or unloved when others say no to us.
- We are annoyed when our desires interfere with others' or when others ignore us, put us down, push us aside, or use us to get what they want.
- As time passes, we learn to treat ourselves the way others have treated us.
- To a degree we will be rejecting of ourselves, living with this hurt, fear, and lie, which will weaken our relationships with God, others, and ourselves.
- Increasingly, we will be oriented to a way of life involving fighting, fleeing, and comforting ourselves, developing addictions, or "worshiping idols."

Rejection in Relationships

- In the vacuum of loving, obtaining what we want is paramount.
- Rejection is the art and craft of using illusion and abusing power to obtain what is desired.
- People may *act like* they each are the authority (God), our judge, claiming to have the truth about our worth, lovability, or capability.

- We may *believe* another person actually is the authority or judge, and we may *believe* his judgments, i.e., the way he treats us has everything to do with us.
- *If* we say or do what the other wants, judgment will be favorable; if we do not say or do what the other wants, judgment will be rejecting.
- Accumulated rejection experiences shape *giver* and *taker* relating styles.
- *Givers* value others and their desires as more important than their own in the hope that others will accept or "like" them and not reject them.
- *Takers* value themselves and their desires as more important than others in order to protect themselves from expected rejection or interference from others to getting what they want.
- Both of these relating styles strengthen self-rejection and deepen the belief and practice of rejection, which is so common that it is accepted as a feature of social reality.
- Rejection is the ultimate source of stress, conflict, trauma, and disease.

With all our hearts, minds, souls, and strength, we must reject rejection in our lives. There is no place for the illusory belief of rejection or the actions it spawns in our relationships with God, others, or ourselves. God does not reject us, even though by way of sin we have rejected Him countless times. Jesus died and rose from the dead to overcome sin and rejection once and for all. No one could ever overcome rejection without Him. He has given us the reason and the power to embrace loving as the only way to obtain what we want with others.

Loving

Respect

Spiritual Respect

- God—the great I AM, the Creator, the Savior, the Holy Spirit leading us all to Him, and the glorious gifts of His love and grace—deserves our purest and most passionate praise, our unrelenting and complete thankfulness, the offering of the life He gave us, and the absolute dedication of our will to follow and serve Him, placing Him above everyone and everything else in our lives.
- Curiously, respecting God will protect us from rejection, harm, fear, doubt, discouragement, helplessness, and hopelessness, while giving us comfort, healing, hope, joy, wisdom, understanding, perspective, strength, patience, truth, determination, peace, trust, faith, and love.

Self-Respect

- You are a child of God (Philippians 2:15); a redeemed person (Isaiah 51:11–12); a forgiven person (1 John 1:9); a new creation (2 Corinthians 5:17); and a victor (Romans 8:35–37).
- *God has given you priceless importance*, equality with everyone, and infinite limitations to keep you humble and engaged with Him and others so that you can love your way through life.
- Value the life and care for the body, mind, heart, and soul that God gave to you, especially when faced with rejection.

Respect in Relationships

- You have the responsibility, honor, and pleasure to respect everyone, at all times.
- You have the right and entitlement to respect from everyone, at all times; ask for it and insist on it for the benefit of others and of your relationships.
- How we treat each other is vastly more important that any desire we will ever have. Let's make a stand together for respect in relationships, in each other, and in ourselves.

Respect God by devoting your every act as praise, thankfulness, and worship and by following His will. Place others above yourself, for your own good and as an encouragement for others to join you in living for Jesus. Treat others and yourself as God treats you, to glorify God.

Loving

Peacemaking

Spiritual Peace

- "Peace I leave with you; My peace I give you. I do not give to you as the world gives. Do not let your hearts be troubled and do not be afraid" (John 14:27).
- "Acquaint now thyself with him, and be at peace: thereby good shall come unto thee" (Job 22:21).
- "He will be called Wonderful Counselor, Mighty God, Everlasting Father, Prince of Peace" (Isaiah 9:6).

Making Peace with Yourself

- Invest time in your relationship with the Prince of Peace, take in the Light of the World, drink the Living Water, read the Word of God (your daily bread), talk with Him and listen (pray), and let Him be your constant companion.
- Stand still, breathe, step into the present moment, clear your mind, and choose to calm down before saying or doing anything.

- Live a practice of forgiveness—seek it from Jesus, receive it fully from Him, and then offer it to and seek it from others.
- Lead by example, speak and act safely, work with and not against others; rather than forcing or pressuring others, invite them to join you in peace.

Making Peace in Relationships

- Proactively plan with everyone close to you that each one of you will take responsibility to calm down in times of conflict and to help the other calm down so that you can work together to resolve conflicts.
- Interrupt "working against" relating patterns (tension, anger, hurt, or fear will be evident) without blaming or rejecting. Be still and quiet until there is calm; ask for a "time-out"; ask the other to describe what she wants; and ask for an agreement to continue peacefully together.
- Repair hurt through forgiveness: take responsibility; empathically listen; express genuine sorrow; make amends; and commit to a peaceful way of acting in the future. Lead by example, and ask others to join you.
- If needed, ask one or two others to help restore peace.

"Blessed are the peacemakers, for they will be called the sons of God" (Matthew 5:9).

Loving

Actively Listen

Spiritual Listening

- "But seek ye first the kingdom of God, and his righteousness, and all these things shall be added unto you" (Matthew 6:33).
- "For I came down from heaven, not to do mine own will, but the will of him that sent me" (John 6:38).
- "'Not by might nor by power, but by My Spirit,' says the LORD of hosts" (Zechariah 4:6). Yield to the Holy Spirit.
- "The fruit of the Spirit is love, joy, peace, longsuffering, kindness, goodness, faithfulness, gentleness, self-control" (Galatians 5:22–23).

Listening Actively

- Be patient; put aside momentarily what you are thinking, feeling, and wanting.

- Ready yourself to seek and receive what the other is thinking, feeling, and wanting. Give your undivided attention. Be present. Make eye contact.
- Listen for the message the person is sending. Acknowledge and affirm the feeling he is conveying. Focus on the desire he has in the moment. Give importance to accurately receiving what he is sending. Don't give importance to "noise," which is a form of rejection. Be careful not to make assumptions or "mind read." Reflect and ask questions to clarify.

Actively Listening in Relationships

- Propose slowing down and making sure we help each other to listen and understand.
- Be willing to listen first. Hear out what the person has to say, reflecting back to her; using her words to reflect what she thinks, feels, and wants; and asking for clarification until she confirms that you've got it.
- Seek specificity, simplicity, and truth in positive, descriptive statements of what the person wants to see happen.
- If the message is getting too complex or running on, ask to take one thing at a time. Ask if she would like to hear your reaction before she moves on to another part of her message. Consider resolutions together for each part of any complex message, or come to an agreement about how to deal with the various parts of the complex message before going over each part in detail.

My beloved brethren, let every man be swift to
hear, slow to speak, slow to wrath ...
(James 1:19).

Loving

Expressing Desires

Spiritual Expression of Desires

- Love the LORD your God with all your heart, mind, soul, and strength, and others as yourself. This is what God wants; this is His will. He puts it first, above any of our desires.
- God's will shall be done for your protection, your benefit, and His glory.
- Be cautious of any desire that is not in line with the Great Commandment.
- "Until now, you have not asked for anything in my name. Ask, and you will receive, and your joy will be complete" (John 16:24).
- "What do you want?" Even though Jesus knew the answers, he repeatedly asked this question to emphasize the importance of seeking *and* giving this information to one another in the spirit of love.

Self-Expression of Desires

- Every moment, desires surface into everyone's awareness, drawing us to take care of them.
- Because desires pose a risk of conflict, many are not spoken; missing ("I don't know"); evasively stated in the form of vague, abstract generalizations (intending to avoid conflict yet ironically provoking conflict); or stated in a negative form (confrontation) in an attempt to remove barriers to desires.
- It is important to be aware of both our own *and* others desires, acknowledging them and expressing them in a "here and now," descriptive, specific, positive statement of exactly what we want to see happen.

Expressing Desires in Relationships

- Give priority and focus to desires in relationships, both others' and your own.
- Be prepared to help others and yourself to describe clearly and exactly what you want to see happen.
- Ask others or yourself to calmly reflect with an open mind on what truly is desired right now. Value it as important, and share it when it comes to mind.
- Ask others or yourself to visualize the moment when you or they will obtain what is desired, as if in a photograph or a movie, and describe what you or they see in detail at that moment.
- If desires surface in the mind or communication in negative forms (e.g., "Stop," "Don't," or "I don't like it when you …"), ask what you would like to see happen

instead. What would the "happy ending" look like when the desire was satisfied?

*"Delight thyself also in the L*ORD*; and He shall*
give thee the desires of thine heart"
(Psalm 37:4).

Loving

Collaboration

Let's search together for ways to help each other fulfill
our desires and not rest until we are both content.

Spiritual Collaboration

- "All I have is yours and all you have is Mine" (John 17:10a). It is infinitely more important that we take care of our desires together in love than that we get anything we want.
- "Blessed be God ... who comforted us in all our tribulation, that we may be able to comfort them which are in any trouble, by the comfort wherewith we ourselves are comforted of God" (2 Corinthians 1:3). By the grace and love of God we are given our hearts' desires when we believe and love Him. So we are encouraged to take care of our desires in love for His glory and our joy.

- "Jesus, knowing that they intended to come and make Him come by force, withdrew" (John 6:15). Make a stand; insist that desires should be taken care of together in love; and refuse to do it any other way.

Personal Collaboration

- Our nature, our "automatic pilot" or habit, is to pursue moment-to-moment desires alone, as if our happiness depended only on having what we want.
- By our will, or by our deliberate choice, we can step into the present moment, value others' desires as our own, and join with others to explore how everyone's desires can be met in acceptance, respect, and peace.
- Relationships, and everyone in them, will win when there is collaboration, which is the best way to take care of desires, feelings, problems, and conflicts.

Collaboration in Relationships

- Orient each other to the supreme importance of helping one another over individuals getting what they want. Collaboration is complete when everyone is content. Take care of the "goose that lays golden eggs."
- Brainstorm ideas together without critical thinking or critical communication. Play off each others' ideas, and be creative. Play. Take the time you need to get a big pool of ideas. Consider asking others for ideas.
- Without force or pressure, review the ideas together, looking for ways to take care of the desires that will work for everyone.

- Ask and insist that anyone working against you, work with you.

"But by an equality, that now ... your abundance may be supply for their want, that their abundance also may be supply for your want; that there may be equality" (2 Corinthians 8:14).

Appendix II
The Heart of Parenting

Highland
Thomas J. Gaffney, Psy.D.
Psychologist and Founder
E-mail: highlandsanctuary@fairpoint.net
www.mainechristiancare.com

Peace

- Be safe in word and deed, use a soft voice, and be gentle.
- Be a peacemaker and guardian, upholding respect for all.
- Be calm, be quiet, breathe, take care of yourself, and offer/ask/insist that others take time to be calm.
- Be forgiving; seek forgiveness, and offer it.

Love

- Connect with eye contact, smiles, and touch before, during, and after any communication.
- Accept unconditionally—listen for the other person's message, feelings, and desires, and then validate and affirm those desires.
- Give and share what you think, know, believe, and value; what you feel and why; what you want to see happen now; and what your hopes and dreams are.
- Together look for ways to explore and experiment, fulfill desires, take care of feelings, solve problems, and resolve conflicts.
- Join in each other's play and work.

Leading

- Plan ahead together—be proactive. Together set a destination or a goal and consider potential ways of reaching it and potential consequences for each way. Then form the action plan.
- Rehearse together, giving your best performances.
- Lead the way by example.
- Consider together the results: What happened? What worked? What can be done better? What was learned? What next?
- Say, "Let's try again until we are both happy."

Say, "Let's prepare a routine and rehearse it."- for any recurring situation that is difficult.

Saving

- Loving you means "I will do anything to save you from trouble. Would you like me to save you?"
- When it's not working, say, "Let's do something different."
- Say, "Let's have a signal so we can stop, stand still, and breathe," interrupting what is not working. For example, here are possible signals you could say:

"Red light" from the "Red Light, Green Light" game. When we hear "red light," we'll freeze. We will all stop moving and talking, calm down, interrupt our habits, step into the present together, listen for what each person wants, and help each other.

"Have a seat," which could be used when "red light" is passed by: the child goes to a previously chosen seat to interrupt what is happening and to prepare to listen and work together. Say, "Let me know when you are ready to work with me."

"I'm giving you some private time in your room," when having a seat is refused. Quietly, with the least support possible, go with the child to his/her room and before closing the door say, "Let me know when you are ready to come out and have a seat." When ready, the child can have a seat and then let you know when s/he is ready to listen and work together.

- Say, "Change the channel" to suggest changing how the child is viewing (how he is looking at things) and/or doing (how he is acting to take care of what he wants).
- Say, "We will only move on when we have a plan that works for all of us."
- Manage your resources of attention, time, energy, know-how, skill, money, transportation, food, etc., for motivating collaboration. Don't try to control or change your child's behavior. Point out choices and associated consequences.

Guiding/Teaching

- Ask lots of questions; try not to give the answers. Make your children think.
- Give advice only when the children ask for it. "Would you like an idea?"
- Honor choice. Let *natural consequences* do the teaching.
- Do you want me to show you, tell you, or show and tell you? Give information in a way that fits the child and in a way the child can use.
- *Practice* makes perfect; when something is not working, a helpful *consequence* is to practice what could have been done differently, what could have been good for everyone.
- When the child's words or actions violate others' rights for acceptance, respect, fairness, and choice, s/he will need to make *reparations* to make the situation better for others and to redeem herself or himself.

Celebrating

- Show children your joy and pleasure with them.
- Have fun, laugh, joke, be silly together, be dramatic and passionate, and generate excitement often.
- Acknowledge, praise, compliment, and thank your children often.
- Create rituals, ceremonies, and traditions for celebrating accomplishments, child and family milestones, and trials or challenges that have been overcome, great and small.
- Have dinner together every night, have a bedtime routine, say good-byes when separating in the morning, and welcome each other home when you reunite.

"He will carry the Lambs in His arms, holding them close to His heart" (Isaiah 40:11).

Lightning Source UK Ltd.
Milton Keynes UK
UKOW06f2143071215

264264UK00002B/332/P